THE SHADOW OF HIROSHIMA
AND OTHER FILM / POEMS

Tony Harrison was born in Leeds in 1937. His
volumes of poetry include *The Loiners* (winner of the
Geoffrey Faber Memorial Prize), *Continuous*, *v.*
(broadcast on Channel 4 in 1987, winning the Royal
Television Society Award) and *The Gaze of the
Gorgon* (winner of the Whitbread Prize for Poetry).
Recognized as Britain's leading theatre and film poet,
Tony Harrison has written extensively for the National
Theatre, the New York Metropolitan Opera, the BBC,
Channel 4, and for unique ancient spaces in Greece
and Austria. His *Theatre Works 1973–1985* are
published by Penguin and his most recent theatre
works, *The Trackers of Oxyrhynchus*, *Square Rounds*
and *The Common Chorus*, by Faber and Faber. His
film *Black Daisies for the Bride* won the Prix Italia in
1994.

TONY HARRISON
The Shadow of Hiroshima
and other film/poems

Introduced by Peter Symes

faber and faber
LONDON · BOSTON

This collection first published in 1995
by Faber and Faber Limited
3 Queen Square London WC1N 3AU

Phototypeset by Wilmaset Ltd, Birkenhead, Wirral
Printed in England by Clays Ltd, St Ives plc

© Tony Harrison, 1991, 1992, 1995
Introduction © Peter Symes, 1995

'The Gaze of the Gorgon' was first published in *The Gaze of the Gorgon* (Bloodaxe Books, 1992); 'The Blasphemers' Banquet' was first published in *Bloodaxe Critical Anthologies 1: Tony Harrison* (Bloodaxe Books, 1991)

Tony Harrison is hereby identified as author of this work in accordance with Section 77 of the Copyright, Designs and Patents Act 1988

A CIP record for this book
is available from the British Library

ISBN 0–571–17675–5

10 9 8 7 6 5 4 3 2 1

Contents

Introduction

Film is a magical medium. It consists of twenty-four (or in the case of television, twenty-five) flickering images that go to make up one single second. These images, each frozen like a snap in your holiday album, when juxtaposed and run begin to 'move'. The movement is of course an illusion, but it enthrals us. The still images are projected in front of us in a continuous stream, at twenty-four frames a second, and we immediately enter a make-believe world of movement. One second follows the next, and the process of juxtaposition is extended to scenes and amplified with sound, yet at its base lies this formal mechanism of stillness. Of course, if we get it wrong, as happens when we use modern equipment to project silent films that have been shot at a slower speed, the illusion fails and the images become laughable, but few people watching our increasingly dominant visual media ever give this a thought. They watch, and what they see is movement. What better vehicle for a poet to use? Are not the still words, combined into lines, undergoing a similar process, not for the eyes but for the ears? What more exciting process, then, but to combine the two.

Is it this inherent metricality that attracted Tony Harrison into the world of film and television? For years a writer who has worked successfully in the theatre, he has been passionately concerned with the business of making language public, using the stage to do this before he turned his attention to the small screen. His is a public poetry, for public display, something which stems from his classical background and his deep knowledge of Greek drama. It informs much of what he does, and lies at the heart of his efforts. While President of the Classical Association, in 1988, he delivered an address that contains an illuminating insight into this, and into his own assessment of the importance of the poet. Harrison was discussing the Muses, and more particularly his own, commenting that he regarded poetry as being unclassifiable, and impossible to place under the care of any specific Muse from the nine of Greek mythology: 'It's all poetry to me, whether it is for the printed page, or for reading aloud, or for the theatre, or the opera house, or concert hall or even for television.' However, if there were to be one Muse, then it would probably have to be Melpomene, the Muse of Tragedy. He went on to outline why. 'Robert Jay Lifton, the

American professor of psychology, who has charted the effect of the Nazi concentration camps and the nuclear holocaust on our imaginations, and the deeply numbing effect of what must be the most petrifying Medusa-like gaze of all on our sense of futurity, has called for artists to discover a "theatre that can imagine the end of the world and go beyond that . . . [a theatre] that can believe in tomorrow", what he later has to call "a theatre of faith". It sounds to me like a call for the *rebirth* of tragedy. And this theatre he calls for, this tragedy, has to believe in the primacy of the word. I think my obsessive concern with Greek drama isn't about antique reproduction, but part of a search for a new theatricality and also a way of expressing dissatisfaction with the current theatre where I work as a poet.'

It's an interesting statement, giving us hints of Harrison's past, his future, even his motivation. It seems now the most natural thing in the world that he should have gravitated to television, that relentless eye in the corner of our sitting-room that looks at everything and often at nothing, and used it to extend his experiment with theatre and with poetry. Can the use of verse in this context help us to look at the future? Can it also allow us to look at our past and our present with unblinking eyes?

All this talk of Greek drama should not obscure the fact that Harrison's first great love was pantomime, and some of his first experiences of theatre took place in Leeds and Blackpool, cities that he continues to visit and to celebrate. He may return constantly to Greek drama to renew himself, but it is as an English public poet that he works, and one morever concerned to be accessible, as his occasional 'news' items for the *Guardian* newspaper so triumphantly prove. It was not surprising therefore to find ourselves – embarked upon our first television collaboration with Tony, in 1986 – sitting on Blackpool pier with a cast of hungry extras sucking large, skull-shaped lollipops and sticks of rock while he tentatively looked on the bright side of things:

> Life's stick of rock's still got a few sweet licks
> and death lettered right through life can't make it sour,
> so lick your skullicious lollies down to sticks
> and scorn for now the inevitable hour.

*

Since 1936, when Auden took those first tentative poetic steps into
the world of pictures with his famous collaboration on the GPO
documentary film *Night Mail*, there have been a number of poets
brave enough to sup with the devil, daring to combine their poetic
skills with the skills of a film-maker. John Betjeman was perhaps the
most assiduous early practitioner, and there have been others, but it
was not until Tony Harrison turned his attention to the form that
we saw the beginnings of a real development and the creation of a
body of work that actually moved the process onto a different plane.
Here at last was work that was beginning to create its own agenda,
and in which one can discern a development both in form and in
content. It was work that took great risks, and which challenged
many orthodoxies. It brought poetry into the homes of millions of
people, and made it immediate. It was work that truly attempted to
face up to the changing society we live in, and apply to it one of the
oldest art forms in the world – in collaboration with one of the
newest.

In 1986, when I first approached him with the suggestion that he
work on a documentary series about cemeteries to be called *Loving
Memory*, Harrison's work had already appeared several times on the
BBC, and he was about to record his poem *v* for Channel 4, but he
had never been closely involved with a production in a way that
suited him. The experience, however, had equipped him to lay down
some conditions, and his first was so obvious it took us all by
surprise: he would do it, provided *all* the commentary was in verse,
and provided we approached the commission as a true collaboration
– he was no longer interested in producing a few verses to be tacked
onto pictures. I was sitting in a rather dingy Soho restaurant with
my Assistant Producer and Gordon Dickerson, Tony's agent, and I
took a very healthy swig from the wine glass before nervously
assenting. Since no one I knew had ever attempted to drive a full-
length documentary with a verse commentary, I contented myself
with the blissful comfort of ignorance, a comfort that lasted until I
returned to the office to be greeted with the sort of looks and
comments normally associated with a bereavement. Only I think I
was probably the corpse.

But folly occasionally has its own rewards, and a leap into the
dark is wonderful if accompanied by the sort of quatrains (line by
carefully typed line and glued onto pieces of paper) that began to

appear from a room next door to the film cutting-room where
editing on the first film had just started. Tony had not been able to
be present at much of the filming for the series, but he joined us
early enough to influence both the structure and some of the content,
and thus started a process of working that has continued ever since –
a process which involves both enormous commitment from all
concerned and a near total dedication to the finished product on the
part of the poet.

The original idea for a documentary series focusing on various
cemeteries became gradually a meditation upon death, memory, and
the apparent futility of commemoration in the twentieth century. We
were able to plan a beginning that would involve a typical village
churchyard, of the sort familiar to Thomas Gray, so that the metre
of the famous *Elegy* could then provide the poet with a verse form
that he could use throughout. Having decided on the metre, he could
then sit down and think about what needed to be said, and he
started work on the film that eventually ran second in the strand:
Mimmo Perella Non è Piu.

This choice of metre, and its linkage to the subject of the film, has
become a trade mark. So, *The Blasphemers' Banquet* uses the
famous quatrain of Fitzgerald's translation of the *Rubaiyat* of Omar
Khayyam, thus placing that 'Voltaire of the East' centre stage in a
piece about blasphemy. Heine's octosyllabic couplets appear
throughout *The Gaze of the Gorgon*, a film that uses the strange
story about the displacement of a statue of that famous German poet
as the skeleton for an extended essay about war and the twentieth
century. The technique is brought to its logical and dazzling
conclusion in *Black Daisies for the Bride*, when the metres of the
well-known songs that were sung to the people suffering from
Alzheimer's disease became the template for the songs given to the
young brides singing in the hospital corridor. Even the difficult
internal rhymes from that Edwardian hit 'Daisy, Daisy' were
faithfully reproduced.

Having decided upon his metre for *Loving Memory*, Tony was
then able to approach both filming and editing with his framework
embedded in his brain. *Mimmo Perella Non è Piu* is a film about the
strange burial customs that exist in Naples, and as with a great
many documentaries, the structure of the piece was proving difficult.
There was the obvious progression of a funeral process, but a visit to

the location provided a solution that was much more elegant, and that gave us our first experience of the benefits of working with a poet who could supply poetic solutions within a very realistic framework.

Tony was wandering through the large cemetery in Naples when he came across a poster. Upon it, in bald announcement, was the notice that Mimmo Perella *non è piu* – literally, is no more. Seizing this, Mimmo became our central character, never appearing, but nevertheless ever present, standing in whenever needed. The things that happen to other people became the events that will happen to Mimmo. The verse commentary, while offering plenty of factual insights, became a work of the imagination which both binds the film together and provides it with an additional level.

What is more, our poet-presenter was able to produce three quatrains very quickly, which he recorded as a 'piece to camera' in the cemetery. Writing to order during a busy filming schedule is difficult enough in prose – it's something we expect of journalists in the front line, but not of poets. Yet Harrison's brilliant metrical technique allows him to do this. So we have an introduction that manages to suggest the narrative line of the film, with its story of Mimmo's journey, while also managing to touch on the often complex exploration of such issues as purgatory and the transitional progress of the soul after death. In convincing verse. It's as if Harrison is saying – well, why not in verse, and why not from the front line? With its ringing repetitions, it is an introduction that lingers longer in the memory than most things seen on the small screen:

> *Mimmo Perella non è piu*
> Mimmo Perella is no more.
>
> *Mimmo Perella non è piu.*
> Mimmo Perella is no more.
> This gate his body will be carried through
> he walked past into work not days before.
>
> *Mimmo Perella non è piu.*
> Let's follow Mimmo Perella's fate,
> or, rather, not one single fate but two,
> that of the body brought in through this gate

and put under marble in a dark, dry hole
where Vesuvius's soil makes it like leather,
and that other fate, meanwhile, of Mimmo's soul
exposed to an uncertain, otherworldly weather.

Perhaps the most significant discovery during the filming of this first series was that relating to the subjective. When Tony began to describe what he imagined people were thinking, and it worked, we realized we were on to something. The Neapolitan film centres around a strange custom, apparently peculiar to this region, which involves the exhumation of a corpse about two years after burial, and its re-interment in a wall vault. Family members are present at this gruesome ritual, and it provides a moment in the film which was both difficult to record and potentially difficult to screen.

Poetry alters this scene in a number of ways. As we saw earlier, Harrison is a firm believer in verse's ability to face the unfaceable, and there is no doubt it operates here in a very interesting way. It also allows the writer the privilege of becoming personal – of moving from a documentary record into a world justifiably imagined without in any way undermining the reality. When the moment comes to face the corpse, he places the words into the mind of the man's widow, then slips back almost unnoticed into the third person:

Was this the Vincenzo who I slept beside?
Vincenzo Cicatiello non è piu.
Now, now I know you've really died.
Till now I only half-believed it true.

Being seen in such revolting tatters
wouldn't suit him. He was much too proud!
Although he's dead, she still believes it matters
that they make him feel he looks right in his shroud.

I cannot imagine getting away with this in prose, yet here it added a depth and compassion to the film that was intensely moving. It also does something else. For a reason I am not sure I can explain, it *allows* us to watch. Is there a key here for that 'theatre that can imagine the end of the world and go beyond that . . .'?

At the same time, we became aware of some of the problems the process created. The powerful metre often fought with the picture cuts. The verbal imagery sometimes cancelled out the visual, and vice versa. Slowly, as the editing progressed, both we on the film side, and Tony in his room next door to the edit-suite, began to find solutions to these. We developed an obsessive way of working, which involved rewriting and recutting on a grand scale. The lines would be recorded, and instantly placed against the film. The film would then be recut. This would often create problems for the verse, which would in its turn be rewritten and re-recorded. Each day the cut would be reassessed – a way of getting the metre of the film into our brains – and then the arduous process would begin all over again. Tony has an admirable approach to his verse, both for television and for the stage. It is written and then *tried out*. Spoken, recorded, played back and so on. It is never sacrosanct. The first quatrains that came to that cutting room in 1986 must have been rewritten endlessly, if they survived at all. What mattered was that they had to work, and work in the context of the whole.

As our methods developed, and we began to realize the exciting possibilities, we discussed ways of *filming* that would also assist the process. What shots worked better than others? Should we stay wide or go for closer shots whose power might interrupt the flow? Would tracks allow us to have longer developing shots, which would in their turn not interrupt the verse metre with visual cuts? And what of sound? Could we use sound more inventively here – perhaps even interweaving the prose words of people filmed in a documentary fashion with the verse?

By the time we were working on the fourth film, eventually titled *Cheating the Void*, the possibilities offered by this technique were plain. In a film that became a tour both of the great European cemeteries and of the European century, we exhumed bodies, reanimated dead singers, interwove for the first time a prose comment made by an interviewee, turned the verse into the first person, used a line from a Jim Morrison song as a conclusion to a quatrain, and supported the verse with a much more inventive sound track than existed in the other films. I have a card still, sent to the cutting-room with a provisional script on one of Tony's very infrequent absences. I think it illustrates the system admirably, while also pointing to the process of discovery that continues to this day:

Herewith a very rough first stab. I can't take it further, till you've taken the next step with it. I think I can then take off from there. I've underlined in red the Jim Morrison bit I'd like edited in [this was the line 'No one here gets out alive!' from the Doors' *Five to One*] and I'd like to experiment a little more with that idea on the spoken bits so that it's like a duet/interview still in metre. It could work very well. I'm going to try some of that with Mr Kemp (stonemason at Kensal Green cemetery) and maybe the girl in Kensal Green, but just go ahead with what there is for now. All this in haste. I look forward to prog 4 and the Blackpool bits. If we can make the intercutting of speech work properly it gives me a way in to something more densely peppered with speaking faces etc . . .

It was two years before we worked together again, and then a chance meeting at the Bristol Old Vic and the kindly services of the Ayatollah Khomeini launched us on *The Blasphemers' Banquet*. This time the documentary was driven much more by a poetic imperative, and became a polemical essay that passionately attacked fundamentalists and their fellow travellers. It was a brave toast from the poet to a writer of prose, the novelist Salman Rushdie, at that time just starting his Iranian-imposed exile from normal society.

The Blasphemers' Banquet remains my favourite of Tony's films, and one that is unjustifiably neglected, perhaps because it plays with political and religious fire in a way the Establishment found unsettling. The controversy surrounding its birth was such that it nearly did not receive a first broadcast, never mind a second, having no less an authority ranged against it than the Archbishop of Canterbury. It was made with a passion born of intense anger in the ridiculously short space of about eight weeks, on a tight budget, and under very difficult circumstances, yet its invention and daring still startle.

I have written elsewhere about this collaboration,* and the way its core was transformed by the poet's ability to respond to events as they happened, but it is worth reiterating here the *practical* aspects of the operation because a work like this has a truly organic growth. At the outset there is often only an idea, or at best a fairly sketchy

---

Bloodaxe Critical Anthologies 1: Tony Harrison, ed. Neil Astley (Bloodaxe Books, 1991)

outline, with possibly one or two central scenes. There is no verse, but there may be several inimitable Harrison notebooks filled with jottings, cuttings and old wine labels. There may also be a starting point unrelated to the work, and in this case Tony had for months been toying with the idea of an opera about fundamentalism, to be called 'Heads in the Sand', based on the religious stonings that had started to take place in Iran. The project remained under that label until transmission, but the idea of singing heads buried in the sand disappeared, sadly, at the outset.

A trip to Bradford was the obvious first move once the film had been commissioned, and in April 1989 we arrived at the site of the now infamous book-burning, and began to uncover a number of rich and ironic possibilities: once-powerful churches reduced to being auction houses or carpet salerooms; a chapel now acting as the Omar Khayyam Tandoori Restaurant; the only new religious building a mosque with a golden dome – powerful weapons for a man who disdained all this talk of the eternal.

Harrison's technique is to start with the initial idea – in this case blasphemy, its importance in our culture, and its place in a specific town in England – and work from that foundation using his extensive reading, enormous amounts of research (much of which may be discarded), and the location. He remains flexible, which means he can take full advantage of events as they unfold, and, as we have seen, his remarkable metrical skill gives him a thoroughly hard-headed approach to the words, discarding verses on the one hand and quickly adapting them on the other as necessary.

Where does this ability originate? At a recent meeting he suggested that it might come from his youth, and his insatiable but undisciplined reading, fuelled by the now famous Thomas Campey, bookseller. Campey's market stall, immortalized in the poet's *ex libris* stickers, offered an extremely eclectic selection, and after devouring each set of purchases Tony would take from each what excited him, discarding the rest. It became a way of reading, and thus of interpretation, that involved a wide but random selection, those selections and their randomness both in choice and in eventual juxtaposition acting as a catalyst upon his imagination. Is it this that underlies the now well-established way he works with film, where an initial idea or event is amplified and embroidered with a variety and artistry that is both personal and very unusual?

Blasphemers almost from its inception, and certainly once we had discovered a church masquerading as a restaurant, was designed around a meal. The meal offered opportunities to extol life-enhancing things, particularly alcohol, and it rapidly included the conceit of the various blasphemers who would not be able to accept their invitations to join in the fun.

A frame now existed for the film, but the nature of the main part of it remained vague, and continued to change even during the edit. To take one example: the piece-to-camera in the Bradford square where Tony miracles *The Satanic Verses* back into his hand while sitting in the very space where it was burnt. This was designed as a sequence that would run much earlier than it does in the finished work. Events changed that.

While filming our two absent French blasphemers, Molière and Voltaire, in Paris, the news broke of the death of the Ayatollah. When the footage of the funeral flickered onto the screens across the world, we knew we had a new beginning, and a beginning that underlined much more forcibly the true nature of fundamentalism. The film took on a darker and more aggressive feel. If the fundamentalists could attack us, why could not we, the inheritors of the European rational tradition, attack in our turn? We did so simply by repeating the footage, enhanced here and there either by an occasional trick like slow motion or enlargement, or by a dazzling score composed by Dominic Muldowney. The poet is nowhere to be heard. Instead he chooses to let the image do the work, and only towards the very end do his words emerge, not as a quatrain, but as a heart-breaking refrain given to his wife, the soprano Teresa Stratas, singing of her love for this fleeting life. The refrain, an English translation of a phrase from the Koran, is a Harrisonian inversion. In its original context the phrase is used to warn against attachment to the world. Here it has been appropriated and turned into a hymn of praise for everything fleeting and lovely in this life.

That is an example of the poet leaving well alone, and using the image to telling effect. At the same time, we had started to experiment with techniques that would work better with the verse commentary, and been particularly careful to use longer static and moving shots. One way of achieving a good moving shot in films is to lay a track down, something resembling a railway line, upon

which you can then place a set of wheels for your camera. This we
did on several locations, most notably in a little back alley in
Bradford. One particular shot starts on an obscene scrawl painted
on a boarded up door, and travels from it across a wall, over an
Urdu notice, along a fence, ending finally on the dome of an
unfinished mosque. In the finished film it covers four quatrains, and
allows an unstoppable momentum to build up in the verse that then
continues into the wonderful meditation on transience that lies at the
heart of the piece. None of the quatrains that later accompany this
shot had been written when we filmed it, but nevertheless the ghost
of the metre determined the way in which it was filmed. We had
begun to trust each other – on the one hand I would film sometimes
disconnected and strange shots with a new-found confidence that
they would be connected in the end, and on the other Tony had
started to discover what the armoury of film techniques could offer
him.

The sequence in which this shot occurs starts with a shot of two
beautiful young girls before cutting to a close shot of the graffiti:
'Scarface bummed his Dad . . .'. It is graffiti typical of any wall in
any city:

> Beautiful sisters in their white and green
> innocent of what these crude words mean
> but maybe they will soon discover beauty
> is inescapably bound up with the obscene.

The tracking shot starts at the beginning of the next verse, with a
wider framing of the preceding shot. The movement starts by
hugging the ground, moving over the rubbish and along the fence
before soaring towards the mosque, allowing us to cut to the hill
above the city and visually swoop back down again to the next
location, the auction rooms of David Bishop. The whole sequence,
extending through the seven stanzas following that quoted above, is
almost completely covered by the two shots, the first a track and the
second a pan and zoom. The verse soars alongside them – see pages
59–60 of this book – and this heady mixture, coming at a crucial
moment in the film, proves to be very powerful.

I have dwelt on this film because it illustrates so clearly the ability
of this writer to use his adopted medium. To know when to speak,
of course, but equally important when to remain silent. It is both a

polemic, a powerful film, and wonderful poetry, and it allowed us to continue on our journey of discovery, the sequence quoted being a notable example.

The Gaze of the Gorgon was Tony Harrison's next television work, and it was transmitted on BBC2 on 3 October 1992. It was a single work that had originally been planned as part of a trilogy, the first part in Corfu being a film about the Kaiser, the excavation of a Gorgon's head, and the start of what was to become a very bloody century. Part two moved to Florida, to the town of Arcadia, which Tony had discovered had once possessed the only rattlesnake canning factory in the world. At the same time as these beautiful if deadly snakes were being decimated as a gimmick for tourists, at a nearby airport tests on the first flying bomb were taking place. The second film was intended to cover, from this very particular perspective, the middle years of the century, though containing its hint of Cruise. Part three moved to Frankfurt, with the sequence which now introduces the completed film, and was designed to bring us up to date.

Omitting the rattlesnakes was painful, but with the help of Heinrich Heine, whose statue stands in Frankfurt, and once stood in Corfu, Tony was able to weave together a number of these strands into a film which is a powerful and very personal overview of the twentieth century. It illustrates very clearly the earlier remark about poetry's ability to look unflinchingly at the unbearable. And it took the technique on into several new areas, most notably the use of the Schumann song, '*Was will die einsame Träne?*', which is woven through the film, both sung in German, played in various arrangements and finally rewritten by Tony and sung in English at the conclusion:

> The closing century's shadow
> has darkened all our years
> and still the Gorgon's filling
> my empty sockets with tears.

'*Was will die einsame Träne?*' was written by Heine and set to music by Schumann. When the Empress Elizabeth of Austria built a palace on Corfu she commissioned a statue of Heine, and he was sculpted clutching the text of this poem in his left hand. Strangely, for a member of the Establishment, the Empress had taken a fancy to this dissident Jewish poet, but when the German Kaiser arrived to take possession of her summer retreat after her assassination, Heine was the first person he evicted. The statue, shipped back to Germany, occupied an ignoble position in a coffee house before being moved again when the Nazis started to deface it. It stands now in a little park in Toulon, virtually unknown and unrecognized, having survived the war hidden in a crate. Heine becomes the guide for the film, and his octosyllabic form is used as a metrical template.

Once established in Corfu, the Kaiser decided to play at archaeology, and it was during his time there before the start of the First World War that a large head of a Gorgon was unearthed, part of an early Greek temple. The film/poem takes this creature who turns men to stone as a metaphor for what was being unleashed upon our century. The Gorgon's shadow is with us still, even in the frozen eyes of the drug addicts in the Frankfurt square.

The Gaze of the Gorgon is a difficult work which does not speak to everyone, but it manages to do something I talked about at the beginning of this introduction, and a letter from a viewer might illuminate this more, because it underlines the value and the power of the poetry to speak to us about the unspeakable:

> I don't know if it is the theme which is so strong and hits right at the heart and guts, or the power of the imagery which I can't seem to forget and which jumps out in my mind so vividly. I don't think I have seen anything on fascism that touched and excited me so and at the same time gave me hope. Usually films on the subject leave me depressed, while the *Gaze* left me with a sense of understanding, of facing up to that overpowering threat of fascism; fascism particularly as it is manifested all around us – yes, in the architecture and in things we take for granted and which intimidate and brainwash us – which often paralyse me and make me shrink. Perhaps this is because you can sense the intelligent individual standing so calmly but also so clearly and surely on the other front, making their statement and passing it on to those of us who allow themselves to be intimidated and overpowered by what we see and what we often feel is beyond our strength to stop or reverse.

The statue of a warlike Achilles raised on Corfu by the Kaiser was one such fascistic emblem dwelt on in the film. In the early days of research, before we knew we would concentrate solely on the Greek island, we had been looking at statues of Achilles in this country. I have another cherished postcard from Tony which arrived while we were amassing this research. It shows a photo of Achilles in Hyde Park with a large CND poster attached to his infamous figleaf. On the back Tony has written: 'We should collect the different signs covering the cock of Achilles. I have one "No War in the Gulf". Can researcher acquire as many as possible?' We duly acquired as many cocks as we could lay our hands on, but in the end the only one that illuminated the film is the one on the Kaiser's statue, another example of the Harrisonian research method. As if to appease us, however, this cock did have a covering of sorts, something picked up by the eagle-eyed poet on our first visit to the island:

> this bellicose, Berlin-gazing totem
> has hornets nesting in his scrotum.

The Harrison style has been pushed furthest in his portrait of Alzheimer's disease sufferers, *Black Daisies for the Bride.* * Completed and transmitted in 1993, the verse in this film, unlike his other films, was given to performers (to sing). (*A Maybe Day in Kazakhstan* was conceived for Melina Mercouri, but she died before she could perform for the film.)

Here again, the techniques developed elsewhere come into play. The intense research (including extensive work with all the families concerned), followed by a documentary filming period of two weeks during which time the world of Whernside Ward at High Royds Hospital, Menston, West Yorkshire, was recorded. Then an initial post-production period for documentary editing and writing. At this stage, the composer Dominic Muldowney became involved, and the period was followed by music recordings, casting and rehearsals. The 'drama' shoot was next, taking place over another eight days, and we returned to the cutting rooms to edit, and to write 'commentary' (also sung), Tony now having decided he could do this using the metrical vehicle of 'In the Bleak Mid-Winter'. Further recordings, using schoolchildren from Menston, followed, and the

---

Black Daisies for the Bride (Faber and Faber, 1993)

whole was then completed with sound mixes, film printing and on-line editing.

This time a very different thing was being attempted. For the first time in his work, we were going to interweave performance with documentary, and we were going to do it in an ethically difficult arena. Yet it seemed the only way to offer an insight into the world of the sufferers, placing them centre stage, without the intervention of professionals in white coats, while at the same time allowing us to give the viewer a hint of their past lives.

At the same time, Tony had decided to use the music heard on the ward, or discovered in the past lives of the patients, as his template, and so the first editing period found him struggling with words that had to fit into models as diverse as 'Oh, You Beautiful Doll' and Puccini's *Madame Butterfly*. The achievement of putting colloquial words into the operatic framework of Puccini was particularly exciting, and was then carried forward by Dominic Muldowney using musical fragments of the opera as a frame. More than most, this work is unclassifiable. I suspect that Tony's failure to fit into a neat pigeonhole may be one of the reasons we never seem to see the films more than once. *Daisies* has proved no exception, and when it received two awards, one was for being the best documentary and the other for being the best drama!

Since *Black Daisies for the Bride* Tony has worked on two films for Channel 4, *A Maybe Day in Kazakhstan* and *The Shadow of Hiroshima*. The first he co-directed with Mark Kidel, but the latter he directed himself, and both films contain developments upon the earlier work: the use of synchronous contributions from bystanders that are woven into the verse; the use of music and sound as integral to the whole (some of it emanating from the documentary, the sound even being recorded by the poet or, in the case of *The Shadow of Hiroshima*, by the composer, Richard Blackford, taken on location to act as the sound recordist); the playful and clever transformation, in the verse, of documentary material discovered on location. Hard to forget the witty use of a Trotsky lookalike doll with revolving eyes to make fun of the Soviet ideal of permanent revolution in *Kazakhstan*:

> there, in strange surgical disguise,
> Dr Trotsky rolls his eyes
> drinking his prescribed solution,

> only his eyes in revolution
> and that by no means permanent
> once Dr Trotsky's battery's spent.

The Shadow of Hiroshima in one way brings us back full circle to *Loving Memory*. When it was transmitted on 6 August 1987, the episode *Cheating the Void*, which starts in Père Lachaise cemetery in Paris and passes through twentieth-century Europe to the firestorms of the bombed city of Hamburg, left the question of total annihilation open, though it was very much at the forefront of Tony's thoughts.

Cheating the Void started with Lumière's famous film of factory workers leaving their workplace:

> These people are all dead, and yet they walk.
> The first in fact to move on celluloid.
> Though they are silent and won't ever talk
> their very movements seemed to cheat the void.

The Shadow of Hiroshima also starts with a shadow, though this time not a celluloid one, but the burnt outline of a man whose body has been photographed, not by celluloid, but by stone. He is one of many thousands killed by the atomic bomb dropped on Hiroshima in 1945, and Harrison gives him a voice, and a lover, in a film/poem of great emotional intensity. Like Heine before him, Shadow-san becomes our guide, and his story (and longing for an ordinary life) is interwoven into the build-up for the annual ceremony of releasing the 'doves' that takes place beneath the famous Peace Dome in the city. The doves are in fact pigeons, and they form the other major strand in the film, as we follow them and their keepers, including Shadow-san, from their cages to the park and then, for the lucky ones not savaged by the Hiroshima hawks, home again.

The other presence in the film is that of the A-bomb Peace Dome, the famous Hiroshima landmark that is the only remnant from the old city. Tony had originally planned to do a work that featured this exclusively, a kind of 'One Hundred Views' like the famous views of Mount Fuji by the painter Hokusai, and while that idea changed, nevertheless the building is an unsettling presence throughout the film, caught in the back of shots, reflected in the water, seen through the windows of the NHK. For this film the poet became director, and his composer Richard Blackford became the sound recordist, capturing effects which he later uses in his music to telling effect (as in the wonderful baseball sequence). It is a fitting film to open this collection with, and one which amply demonstrates the distance that Tony and his collaborators have travelled since those first halting steps in a cutting room in Bristol struggling to make a film about bodies being exhumed by Neapolitans.

When Auden commenced work on his first effort in this field over half a century ago, he little realized how much further his successor would develop it. Auden's *Night Mail*, and his thoughts about verse and film which he made public in a lecture to the North London Film Society remain tantalizingly prophetic, and his conclusion is still relevant for us today.* Having outlined what he saw as the advantages and disadvantages of verse and film (he saw the collaboration as offering distinct possibilities), Auden ended by pointing out that the most difficult element in the equation was finding the right kind of support, both financial and artistic, to enable this process to develop. As I have tried to show here, that development may often take place over an extended period of time, and require a great deal of faith. It may well be that poets need to either learn the business themselves, or develop their skills in conjunction with a compatible film-maker. What is certain is that if it is to work this form is something that must be allowed a life of its own, with the space to grow. None of this would have happened if the poet had not been allowed the room to develop and experiment.

Composers are often regarded by the film-making establishment as people to call on to fill a few gaps. Too rarely are they used in a truly collaborative manner. Similarly I suspect that if used at all, poets are viewed in a similar way, called on to decorate a vacancy that exists in the film, and sadly in the film-maker too. But it is no longer possible to say that poets cannot or should not work on film. Harrison's work alone has confounded that argument. All that is needed is the means to continue the work, and the critical faculties to analyse it properly.

The scripts assembled in this collection, ranging from work done in 1986 through to Harrison's most recent film/poem for Channel 4 in 1995, deserve to be preserved. Reading them is a poor substitute

*W. H. Auden and Christopher Isherwood, *Plays and other Dramatic Writings 1928–1938*, ed. Edward Mendelson (Faber and Faber, 1989)

for *seeing* and *hearing* them, but even in the age of the VHS and the laser disc getting hold of these films is easier said than done, and at the very least being able to study them on the printed page will give a sense of the diversity and range of the work. As you read them, never forget that this is work that is designed to be *seen* and *heard*. It has been specially constructed with pictures in mind. It is specially commissioned work, written and rewritten with much trial and error both at the filming and the editing stages, created with often painstaking experiment. Almost as much as survives upon these pages lies on the cutting room floor.

It has been written only so that it could exist alongside those other elements that go to make up a film – the pictures, obviously, but also the other sounds ranging from synchronous prose to sung music. It is not for nothing that Harrison has chosen to call his works film/poems, and his willingness to work in this way may seem to many writers to be brave, but to me it seems quite natural that he should find himself working in this many-layered medium. Maybe it is the classical education, or those pantomimes, or Thomas Campey or even Frank Randle – whatever the mix, the resulting chemistry has provided us with a film-poet of outstanding versatility and power.

Peter Symes

THE SHADOW OF HIROSHIMA

The Shadow of Hiroshima was first broadcast on Channel 4
on 6 August 1995.

Sound Programmer Glenn Keiles
Research Assistant Sarah Bhathena
Assistant Producers Alison Carter, Diane Holmes
Telecine Grading Colin Peters, Luke Rainey
On-line Editor Adam Grant
Dubbing Mixer Nick Rogers
Hiroshima Location Manager Keiko Ogura
London Location Manager Dan Leon
Camera Assistant Jack Holmes
Film Editor Luke Dunkley
Sound and Music Richard Blackford
Lighting Cameraman Alistair Cameron
Executive Producer Michael Kustow
Producer Andrew Holmes

Written and directed by Tony Harrison

I heard a sound I thought was birds
but then I swear I heard these words:

SHADOW SAN 'This voice comes from the shadow cast
by Hiroshima's A-bomb blast.
The sound you hear inside this case
is of a man who fans the face
he used to have before the flash
turned face and body into ash.
I am the nameless fanning man
you may address as Shadow San.

The inferno flayed me as I fanned,
gold fan with cranes on in my hand.
In that fierce force but one degree
of quicker combustibility
separated fan and me,
but that one degree meant that the man
was stamped on stone but not the fan.

My shadow's fading and I fear
I may not make centenary year,
and so before I finally fade
give one last outing to this shade,
and you will be my eyes to see
this fiftieth anniversary.'

He bowed. I bowed, and then began
one day's parole for Shadow San.

                    *

Radio exercises   The Shadow said, 'I recognize
this pre-war tune for exercise.
Not only here but through Japan
this was how each day began
with music from the NHK
[our BBC] to start the day.
This Radio Tai-chi's been broadcast
before and since the A-bomb blast.
Radio Tai-chi's brought the nation,
ruined and wrecked, regeneration

of weary flesh and hopeless soul
and got the flag back up the pole.

My shadow's eighty, so is this
devastated edifice,
built 1915 by a Czech
A-Bomb Dome   now A-Bomb Dome, symbolic wreck
left standing for our meditation
on nuclear death and devastation.

Though the river by the name
of Motoyasu's just the same
and though the old sun emblem flies
there's nothing else I recognize
in all this city I called home
but this gaunt husk, this gutted Dome
opposite the Peace Park where
they'll loose the doves into the air
tomorrow at 8.23
too late, alas, for me to see.
At 8.15 the Peace Bell's chime
means my fiftieth burning time.

*

KOBAISHI, SAN   Kobaishi San,
Hiroshima's champion pigeon man,
does Radio Tai-chi exercises
beside his pigeon racing prizes
and cooing and flapping up above's
a loft full of symbolic doves
his pigeons are called on to be
tomorrow at 8.23.
August 6th, 8.23's
the time tomorrow that makes these
flapping pigeons VIPs.
Kobaishi San's cohort
of colombophiles, apart from sport,
every August 6th supply
doves of peace to fill the sky
at 8.23: eight minutes past

the time of Hiroshima's A-bomb blast.
And all the homing pigeons home
back to their lofts past A-Bomb Dome.
He'll be there to count them back and by
about 8.30 he can scan the sky
and at 8.40 can begin
to whistle his flock of pigeons in.

*

The Flame of Peace burns just behind
the ten green cages where, confined
until tomorrow's special day,
the pigeon fanciers' peace doves stay,
kept unfed, till they're set free
tomorrow at 8.23,
and, in about ten minutes, speed
back to their lofts to get their feed.

*

SAKAMOTO SAN

And this is Sakamoto San,
proud his birds can help Japan
make tomorrow's plea for Peace,
who crates a score for the Release.
And he'll be at his loft to count,
if twenty go, the same amount
come home. Though the flight back's short
peace doves can get lost, or caught.

*

Hara San paints
the A-Bomb
Dome

While pigeon fanciers prepare
others start the day with prayer.
Like Hiroshi Hara who each year
begins his own peace ritual here.
'Hiroshi Hara, did you say?'
said Shadow San, 'Alive today?
How come a man now sixty-three
survived the Bomb blast and not me?'

TONY HARRISON

Because, by chance, he was away
at his grandmother's that fatal day,
Hara San has lived to see
this fiftieth anniversary.
Hara San, lucky to survive
and live to 1995,
is a painter and his way
of commemorating A-Bomb Day
and all his friends lost in the war
is on the 5th, today, to draw
and paint the A-Bomb Dome with water from
the river those flayed by the Bomb,
including all his friends from school,
jumped in, hoping it would cool
their burning and bomb-blackened skin,
here where he dips his bottle in.
His schoolmates' shrieks from blackened lips
haunt Hara San each time he dips
his brush in water from the stream
to give relief to those who scream,
all his dying schoolmates, those
whose skin slid off their flesh like clothes.
Like clothes, three sizes oversize
their flayed skin loosens from their thighs.
Burns and blisters, bloated blebs
burst as the Motoyasu ebbs,
the tidal Motoyasu trails
black flaps of flesh like chiffon veils.
Like kimonos with their belts untied
black sloughed-off skin floats on the tide.
This water mixed with children's cries
paints the Dome, green trees, blue skies
and in that way, he hopes, redeems
something from his schoolmates' screams.
'The force that blew the Dome apart,'
said the Shadow, 'makes short work of art.'

*

Baseball stadium   Close to the Dome on soil where heat
burnt the soles off people's feet,
on Saturdays, close to Ground Zero,
crowds cheer the current sporting hero.

Tomorrow they may pause in play
to watch the peace doves pass that way.

Shadow San stood, head on one side,
listening, and then he cried:
'You'd need a stadium five times higher
to seat all those who died by fire.
Where you see baseball I can hear
all those thousands who can't cheer.
Listen, can't you hear the choir
of those who perished in the fire?'

'I hear a baseball being hit
or thudding into catcher's mitt!'

Shadow San, exasperated
I heard no chorus of cremated,
deaf to all the humming dead,
turned to me again and said:

'Dead men's mouths make only M,
the M in Do*m*e, the M in Bo*m*b,
tuned to the hum that's coming from
the A-Bomb Dome that I hear hum
all round this baseball stadium,
still after all these fifty years
reverberating in my ears.
Can you *not* hear it? Or the choir?'

'No, only a baseball hitting wire!'

And you, in front of your TVs
which are, no doubt, all Japanese,
all you sitting there at home
can you hear the humming Dome,
the M, the M? As one of those
who always haunts where water flows

Shadow San, destroyed by heat,
drew me away to this retreat.

*

Shinto shrine'This,' said Shadow San, 'this shrine,
though I'm not certain, seems like mine.
The fiery fountain dragon felt
the same fierce force that made me melt
and melted but can be remade
to spout cool water in the shade.
Burnt red banners and bamboo,
orange arches all made new.
That character carved on this trough
was blackened but not blasted off.
This lion though its jaw got cracked
has all the rest of it intact.

I came here to this Shinto shrine
most mornings between eight and nine,'
the Shadow told me, 'and the day
I was to die I came to pray,
to pull the bell rope, throw the yen,
bow twice, clap twice' . . . He broke off. Then
Shadow San, although he fanned
obsessively, grabbed at my hand
and with a more than shadow squeeze
made my blood and spirit freeze.
SONOKO'I see my Sonoko returning.
It was her who I was yearning
on the steps for, burning, burning.

Ah those tender, tender fingertips
the memory of those lips, those lips.'
At that moment no dead man
can have longed for life like Shadow San,
who, hoping love could break through time
thought he watched his loved-one climb
the blasted but now rebuilt shrine
to seek the help of powers divine.

But once he'd seen her throw the yen
hope left him when he spoke again.
'No! No!' he said, 'Not Sonoko,
we both died fifty years ago.
And if she *had* survived she'd be
a scarred and shrunken seventy-three.
But that girl, head bowed at the shrine
wrings my heart, she's so like mine,
so like the girl I was to meet
that August 6th and go and eat
sushi and drink *sake* and . . .
the night of love we'd also planned.
And I sat longing, planning
on the bank steps, fanning, fanning
in a 100 Fahrenheit
longing for my girl and night . . .
when all my flesh was set alight.'

*

NHK and
A-Bomb Dome

Above this shrine where he had seen
the girl like his, the workers clean
windows at the NHK
(their BBC) for Peace-Dove Day
and clean the windows so they'll see
to film the peace-doves being set free
or point out to visitors the view
the Shadow keeps returning to:
'The A-Bomb Dome I never can
quite lose from view,' said Shadow San.
'It's as if,' he said, 'these views were by
my favourite painter Hokusai,
and if he re-did his hundred views
instead of Mount Fuji now he'd choose
as Hara San, his painter heir
still painting on his folding chair,
chose, the A-Bomb Dome, the eye
always gets recaptured by.
I take my city bearings from
that fellow relic of the Bomb.'

Elementary
school

The school where all the pupils died
stands rebuilt near this riverside.

*

When Shadow San set eyes on these
he began to sing in Japanese:
'*Misu, misu kudasai,*
water, water they'd all cry
burned and blackened, soon to die
if these pupils here had been
in this same room at 8.15
the 6th of August '45.

None of them would be alive.

And none would see another star
if they'd been where now they are,
and me, this shadow Rip Van Winkle
for whom all stars have lost their twinkle,
came here to school before the War
and also learned to use a saw.

I hear my own voice in this choir
I hope the world will spare from fire.
I learned this song, it's one you sing
to calm little pigeons panicking.'

*

MITSUFUJI SAN

The A-Bomb Dome and all the rest
make Mitsufuji San depressed.
He wouldn't mind if it was made
into a vast pinball arcade,
a game that millions will play
even tomorrow, A-Bomb Day.
He's never been to see you yet,
I told the sullen silhouette.
He thinks it's better to forget.

He likes to sing, to play, to laugh,
never goes near the Cenotaph,
unless, like now, delivering doves.

He only does the things he loves,
what makes him happy, and doves do.
He sings to them to make them coo;
his girlfriend does, and he'd prefer
to sing this little song to her,
a pigeon song he'd sooner use
to calm her flutters into coos.
Shadow San who said he'd seen
birds in flames at 8.15
with a dead man's closed mouth M
hummed the pigeon song with him,
then said quietly, 'Which burns quicker,
birds or basket, wings or wicker?'

Tram crosses the
Aioi Bridge

As the sun-drenched streetcar crossed
the centre of the Holocaust,
the Aioi Bridge the Enola Gay
took focus from that fatal day,
I heard the fanning Shadow say:
'The trams of Hiroshima ran
always on time,' said Shadow San,
'but at 8.15 were blasted black
along this then bomb-buckled track
and all the passengers, like me,
were fanned into eternity.'

Mitsufuji San
phones Sonoko

The Shadow melted into shade.
I thought the phone made him afraid,
I thought the booth put him in mind
of that place he'd been confined
until this morning in and must return
when the Peace Bell chimes to burn
and to resume at 8.15
his most uncarnal quarantine.
Though Mitsufuji hates to dwell
on why and how the A-bomb fell
the Dome's dark hellish silhouette
summons up his dove, his pet.
The fanning shade stood flabbergasted
that the Dome the Bomb had blasted

could now so magically summon,
from waste and wilderness, a woman.

I asked the Shadow to translate:
'The A-Bomb Dome makes him a date
but he's got some hours to wait.
He'll leave his peace-doves first and then
go to play pin-ball until ten.'

*

Hara San paints
the A-Bomb
Dome

Hara San hears scorched throats croak
where now new thirsts get quenched by Coke.
'And Coke,' sighed fanning Shadow San,
'has come to conquer new Japan.'

The forecast from the NHK
predicts another scorching day
tomorrow and the shops will sell
scores of ice-cold crimson cans
of Coke, and scores and scores of fans
to cool the watchers waiting for
the liberated doves to soar.

*

Tomorrow morning, 8.15,
he'll give the trees their August green
and the sky its final blue,
then what Hara San will do
at the very moment the Bomb fell
and he hears the tolling of the bell
is seal and sign it with the date . . .
'The date that also sealed my fate,'
added the watching Shadow San
who, as the day cooled, closed his fan.

Sunset

The setting sun forecast as stronger
tomorrow made my shadow longer,
but Shadow San's stayed just the same
as when first cast by flash and flame.

The sun tomorrow that's forecast
as hot as when the A-bomb blast
exploded fifty years ago
will make the fans flap to and fro
and sell a fortune in iced drinks
but now, turns fiery red, and sinks.

*

Hiroshima by night, neon lights

Except when nightworld neon threw
his outline out in red or blue,
or he made another bitter joke
about the crimson conqueror, Coke,
he stayed unseen and silent in the night
until he stopped me at this sight:

Parlour Atom pinball arcade

'Parlor Atom, look this sign
must mean another A-bomb shrine
with shadows in it just like mine.
Perhaps I'll find a fellow shade.'

'It's a mere pinball machine arcade
I'm sorry to tell you, Shadow San,
there are thousands like it in Japan
there are 30 million Japanese
spend their nights in "shrines" like these.'

'I thought Mitsufuji came to pray!'
'No, Shadow San, to play, to play
A pinball addict I'm afraid.'

We watched him enter the arcade.
The sound unleashed made Shadow shrink.
He shouted out: 'It makes me think
of Hiroshima shattering, and me
a shadow showered with bomb debris.'

*

Mitsufuji San meets Sonoko

Shadow San drew me ahead
half-excited, half in dread,
and when Mitsufuji came he said:

13

'Mitsufuji's little dove
's so like my own cremated love,
and maybe all my dead man's yearning,
still undiminished from the burning
has made Mitsufuji San,
the Hiroshima pigeon man,
and the *sake* girl he's met unite
to commemorate my final night.'

The thought consoled him for a while.
But Shadow San soon lost the smile
I'd imagined that he'd had
and stopped me in the night to add:

'Like men condemned to hang or fry
get favourite meals before they die,
the man who fanned his way to hell
wills them to the Love Hotel.'

*

Mitsufuji San
and Sonoko in
Love Hotel

'Seeing Sonoko asleep
could even make a shadow weep.
Girls as beautiful, as young, as sweet
were seared to cinders by the heat.

Sayonara, Sonoko,
I love you but I have to go
back to my museum case
with no body and no face,
back to a world where none embrace
nor do the things I did before
our hawks and jingos joined the war,
and you're so lucky to do after –
drinking *sake*, singing, laughter,
even Parlor Atom, but above
everything on earth, to love.

Sayonara, I must return
back to the bank steps where I'll burn.
tomorrow morning, 8.15,
only this flimsy paper screen,

flammable as a fan, 's between
your sleeping body and the man
who'll be cremated, Shadow San.
When you hear the Peace Bell chime
that's 8.15, my burning time.
First the conflagration of the fan
then after it the fanning man.

Before my eyes burst from the heat
a blazing dove falls at my feet.'

Shadow San
departs

I saw the saddened shade retire
to face again the flash and fire.

*

Radio exercises.
Mitsufuji San
wakes in Love
Hotel

Mitsufuji San's alarm
that his doves may come to harm
makes him run past A-Bomb Dome
to catch a tram to take him home
across the bridge they call Aioi,
the bomb-aimer of 'Little Boy'
high up in the Enola Gay
fifty years ago today
took focus from where now we see,
walking the upright of the T,

Peace ceremony
begins

two survivors' shadows but
shadows still fixed foot to foot,
two survivors here to find
the special seats they've been assigned
to hear the speeches, pray, and see
precisely at 8.23
all the doves in the release
making their winged plea for peace.

*

The cicadas' dry tattoo
gets quicker towards 8.22.
Fans, like a chorus of quick sighs,
will the doves into the skies.
A white glove poised against the blue

15

signals it's 8.22,
only one minute now before
the liberated doves will soar
above the fans and the cicadas –
Sakamoto San's, Okada's,
and champion Kobaishi San's
and carefree Mitsufuji San's,
flying above the sighing fans.

Once the signaller's white glove
gives the signal, every dove
will rise and fly as cage-doors fall,
crash to the ground, and free them all.

And fanciers wait at home to greet
their hungry peace-doves home to eat.
Normally each fancier's flock
's back and fed by nine o'clock.

Release of doves,
8.23

*

Last dove

The peace-doves have been freed but why
won't this last shaking straggler fly?
Perhaps he's seen what's in the sky.

Hawks

Where peace-doves are the birds of prey
are never very far away.
These hawks cruising the skies
don't care what peace-doves symbolize.
These emblems are mere morsels, meat,
their ripped-out innards good to eat.
Since yesterday the hawks have waited
to see their lunches liberated.
Hiroshima hawks are glad to glut
and gorge themselves on peace-dove gut.

It's not inappropriate birds of prey
are also present on Peace Day.
They could well stand for Japanese
who forced other Asians to their knees.
They stand for a spirit from the past
that moved Japan before the blast,

the old Japan that took Nanking
under its dark, blood-spattered wing,
Japan in her aggressive guise
taking Pearl Harbor by surprise,
the prison camps that made us pray
for any means to bring VJ.

Many doves freed on this day
fall victims to these birds of prey

Mitsufuji San
back at pigeon
loft

and Mitsufuji fears his may.
A dove he sang to might this minute
have a hawk's beak thrusting in it.

Or, turned scavenger, join other strays
from all the former Peace Dove Days,
from '94, 3, 2, 1.
The Peace Park's almost overrun
and the symbol of man's peace-seeking soul
is a matter for city pest control.

And peace doves of the recent past
could end up sterilized, or gassed.

Those symbolic doves that flew
in '91 or '92
in '93 or 4 survive
by fighting these from '95 . . .

A-Bomb Dome
and pigeons

Pigeon/Peace-doves brawl and fight.

Is the world at peace tonight?

Fan

Or are we all like Shadow San
facing inferno with a fan?

A MAYBE DAY IN KAZAKHSTAN

A Maybe Day in Kazakhstan was first broadcast on Channel 4 on 1 May 1994.

Steadicam Operator Alekos Yiannaros
Camera Assistant Linos Meitanis
Sound Recordist Nikos Barounis
Telecine Grading Colin Peters, Luke Rainey
Rostrum Camera Ken Morse
Production Managers Ariane Cotsis, Paul Frift
Assistant Producer Alison Carter
Lighting Cameraman Alistair Cameron
Editor Julian Sabbath
Music Richard Blackford

Executive Producer Michael Kustow
Producer Andrew Holmes
Directed by Mark Kidel and Tony Harrison

Produced in association with the Foundation for Hellenic Culture

Flea-market

A city wall not quite sure where,
no May Day posters plastered there.
Although it's May Day no parade
disturbs the new free world of trade,
only the memory of a choir
and from it one voice rising higher
out of a red doll standing near a

The *lyra* man

man who bows a Black Sea *lyra*.
I seek directions from the man
who welcomes me to 'Kazakhstan!'

What sometimes haunts these traders' looks
are dark nights and days in cattle trucks.

Cold dark deportation trains
still jolt and judder through their brains.

From Black Sea coast to Kazakhstan
cooped up in a cattle van.

Confined to Kazakhstan and far
from Sukhumi and Krasnodar.

May Day comes and haunts a man
with memories of Kazakhstan.

Flag-seller

Red flags he flogs for what he can
once flew high in 'Kazakhstan!'

This flea market that's now free
from surveillance by the KGB,
though things to aid the human eye
take aim, survey or even spy
are all part of this pavement trade
police no longer keep surveyed.
The free market, seller/buyer
of tablecloths and *Stolichnaya*,
hats made of Siberian furs,
and surplus Soviet secateurs
we see flea-market browsers feel
to test the sharpness of the steel.

Maybe they once cut the wire
that put barbed confines round a choir,
not for pruning plants but man
collectivized in Kazakhstan.

Red dolls

They seem to sell these everywhere
as talismans against despair,
these little dolls on every stall
no force seems able to make fall.
The doll, no matter what the drop, 'll
come up trilling from her topple,
cling to her song and go on clinging
though Kazakhstan could crush her singing,
collectivized and forced by rote
to still the *lyra* in her throat.

Tools and spare parts

We see in these flea-market scenes
all the system's stilled machines,
the bit, the drill, the cog, the gear,
the technology of yesteryear.
The hammer once gripped in the fist
of Stakhanovite and Stalinist
or cast in gold as an award
for greater output quotas scored.
The Stakhanovites have all downed tools
and live by new free-market rules.
And no red flags to stitch or darn
means surpluses of scarlet yarn.

Red Army uniforms

The people's flags of deepest red
novel coverlets to drape a bed.
And uniforms have been sloughed off,
redundant after Gorbachev,
mere novelties a trader peddles,
not in Red Square impaled with medals
bouncing on breasts as brass bands play
marchers and missiles through May Day

This march-past's only shoppers' feet
browsing on flea-market street
in various shoes, high heels or suede,
not in black boots and on parade.

Old woman knitting	She sees their feet from where she's sitting on the pavement, peddling, knitting. And maybe all her bright bootees will walk to better times than these, not crash their heels to May Day brass as medalled smilers watch them pass, not keep in step, or form in ranks and march as boots in front of tanks. And maybe the head that wears this bonnet won't ever need a gas mask on it . . .

Gas masks

The Kazakhstan these masks come from
was the test site for the Soviet bomb.
And choristers in gas masks gag
and can't perform the People's Flag.
The most you'll ever get from them
's a fearful muffled requiem.
The metronome these masks employ
gets sold here as a gruesome toy.

Radiation meters

These meters dumped in great amounts
measure radiation counts.

Army issue anti-gas
and army surplus May Day brass
some Kazakh or Uzbek brigade
marched past with playing on parade.

They need a new tune to redeem
the redness of the old regime.

Toy xylophone

The tune we hear three browsers play
still haunts them though it's had its day.

Pavement peddlers trading trash
from Communism's fatal crash,
salvaging the washed up cargo
from their ill-fated, shattered *Argo*,
spewing from its kitsch-crammed hold
debris to be bought and sold,
and all that spewed-up spillage sprawls
on these pathetic pavement stalls.

23

Doomed Argonauts condemned to peddle
the bric-à-brac of badge and medal
from that doomed voyage that maroons
Lenin here with fork and spoons,
cast in bronze now cast away
to read *Das Kapital* all day.
Most stalls sell his statuette
(though I haven't seen one bought here yet),
this mannikin time's mummified
in philosophical formaldehyde,
and behind bronze Vladimir Ilyich
(once you've pressed his little switch)
there, in strange surgical disguise,
Dr Trotsky rolls his eyes
drinking his prescribed solution,
only his eyes in revolution
and that by no means permanent
once Dr Trotsky's battery's spent.
And Trotsky drinks and drinks and drinks
because the new free market stinks.
Though New World Order mongers crow
that History's got nowhere to go
and make the socialist despair
it's ever going anywhere,
the New World Order thinks we're wiser
when every man's a merchandiser.
But Trotsky goes on making toasts
to *glasnost* and the gulag ghosts.
The foundered *Argo*'s former crew
now peddling here on pavements new,
marooned in free flea-market forces
with no sights fixed on future courses,
what new horizons do they scan,
these castaways from Kazakhstan?

They scan the market where they are,
not Sukhumi or Krasnodar . . .
and not Georgia, Georgia Tblis
(Tblisi, Georgia) but Greece –
not the Black Sea coast Sukhum

Lenin
Trotsky

but to Athens, Greece that they've all come.
This market wasn't Kazakhstan
but where democracy began
Acropolis   two millennia and a half ago
which makes its progress pretty slow.

Athinas Street, This flea-market Athens street
Athens   is where a dream and nightmare meet.
These peddlers, Greeks, once deportees
to Kazakhstan, call Kleisthenes,
democracy's first dreamer, kin
(a dream they want including in)
so come to Greece to reconnect
and salvage lives that Stalin wrecked
and get to feel like Greeks again,
though Greeks still call them Soviet men,
forced out of Georgia and displaced
from fertile farms to barren waste,
at two hours' notice packed in trains
to Central Asia's arid plains.

Archive. Song *'Forced from our farm in Sukhumi*
(tune: 'Red   *though full of tears my eyes could see*
Flag')   *the cotton glow, a golden fleece*
cold in moonlight far from Greece.

Though long ago I've not forgotten
the moonglow on the Kazakh cotton
when we staggered from the cattle van
collectivized in Kazakhstan.'

Their nightmares in the old regime
have not quite dimmed the ancient dream.

Tubas   Two Soviet tubas, silver, brass,
struggle through the May Day mass,
tubas in whose bulled-up gleam
red flags blazoned the regime,
tubas in which bazookas shone
reflecting coats with medals on,
tubas with missiles mirrored in,
now, unregimented, can begin

25

to learn a new tune for today
and play a fanfare not for May
but Maybe Day and that maybe
's the future of democracy.

Procession up
Acropolis Two tubas join their band to blow
as jaunty a new *Jubilo*
as may be hazarded in days
when only a muffled fanfare plays.

This band of Greeks who get called Russian
with their strings, brass and percussion,
whatever they could buy or borrow
(and sell on their own stalls tomorrow)
will play a cautious fanfare blown
for democracy's foundation stone.

Fanfare to
Parthenon They'll wake what may be from the waste,
this makeshift band of the displaced.

Not marble but millennia weigh
on cables that maybe'll fray.
Depending how you calculate
democracy's foundation date
is 506 or 7 or 8
but once you've got it off the ground
with gleeful or more grating sound
and got it hoisted in the air,
it goes into which structure? Where?

With democracy the truth is this:
no final fanfared edifice,
only the crane however grating
continually recreating . . .

Girl in Theatre
of Dionysus.
Lyra player The people's flags of deepest red
spread for tender feet to tread.
Those scarlet standards he saw fly
above his and other heads, held high
in Kazakhstan, when he was Russian,
now he's Greek he watches cushion

the girl's first cautious tread
onto the path of fallen red.

GIRL (song)

'From Kazakhstan now back in Greece
I dream the maybe, piece by piece.
I dream with open eyes and see
the marble of maybe . . . maybe.'

Wide shot,
Theatre of
Dionysus. Fade

The scarlet banners she trod on
to find her red doll have all gone
with all the instruments that played
back into flea-market trade,
the red flags back on pavement stalls,
folded, as May Day evening falls.

27

THE GAZE OF THE GORGON

The Gaze of the Gorgon was first broadcast on BBC2
on 3 October 1992.

Composer Martin Kiszko
Soprano Angela Tunstall
Photography Mike Fox
Sound Recordist Trevor Gosling
Dubbing Mixer Peter Hicks
Dubbing Editor Sue Goodsall
Research Gail Taylor
Additional Research Gerald Lorenz
Production Secretary Anita Gol
Production Manager Valerie Mitchell
Film Editor Liz Thoyts

Directed by Peter Symes

[Lines within square brackets were not included in the broadcast film.]

Exactly a hundred years ago in 1892 the marble statue of a dissident German Jewish poet, rejected by his fatherland, was taken by Elizabeth, Empress of Austria, to a retreat in Corfu. The film-poem follows its fortunes through the century from its eviction from the island by the German Kaiser, who bought the palace after the Empress was assassinated in 1899, to its present resting place at Toulon in France.

Once established in Corfu, the Kaiser claimed that while Europe was preparing for war he was excavating the fifth century BC pediment which featured a giant Gorgon. The film-poem takes this terrifying creature of legend who turns men to stone as a metaphor for what the Kaiser unearthed on to our century, and finds her long shadow still cast across its closing years.

Clutched in the left hand of the marble Heinrich Heine the Kaiser evicted from Corfu is the manuscript of '*Was will die einsame Träne*', a *lied* set to music by Schumann. The song in various transformations makes the same journey as its hounded author.

To the same degree, though in different fashion, those who use force and those who endure it are turned to stone.

Simone Weil: *The Iliad, or the Poem of Force*

Art forces us to gaze into the horror of existence, yet without being turned to stone by the vision.

Friedrich Nietzsche: *The Birth of Tragedy*

Ask General Schwarzkopf who Goethe and Schiller and Heine were. He would be well advised to answer if he wants to go on addressing Chambers of Commerce at $50,000 a pop. 'Were they the outfield of the St Louis Cardinals in 1939?'

Kurt Vonnegut

Gulf: Tank Gorgon / Golden Sea	From long ago the Gorgon's gaze stares through time into our days. Under seas, as slow as oil the Gorgon's snaky tresses coil. The Gorgon under the golden tide brings ghettos, gulags, genocide.

Gulf: Tank
Gorgon / Golden
Sea

From long ago the Gorgon's gaze
stares through time into our days.
Under seas, as slow as oil
the Gorgon's snaky tresses coil.
The Gorgon under the golden tide
brings ghettos, gulags, genocide.

ECU-Land
(Frankfurt)

That's maybe the reason why
so many mirrors reach so high
into the modern Frankfurt sky.

ECU-land seems to prepare
to neutralize the Gorgon's stare.
But what polished shields can neutralize
those ancient petrifying eyes?

Goethe statue,
Frankfurt

Great German soul, most famed Frankfurter
on his plinth, the poet Goethe.
Born Frankfurt but deceased Weimar
where his mortal remnants are.
The old Cold War used to divide
where he was born from where he died
but now they're once more unified.

Schiller statue

And once more it doesn't seem so far
from Frankfurt-am-Main back to Weimar.
And but an amble down an avenue
to Friedrich Schiller on full view
and I suppose I ought to say
it's right they're put on proud display
(though often scorned although their scale
's, say fifty times this can of ale).
It's proper that the Fatherland
should give them monuments so grand
but there's another German who
is quite the equal of those two
(and greater in some people's eyes!),
whose monument's a fifth their size.

HEINRICH
HEINE memorial

There are, I think, three reasons why
my statue's not so bloody high:

1: I was subversive; 2:
(what's worse to some) I was a Jew
and 3: I'm back here almost hidden
because I was ten years bed-ridden
with syphilis; this keep-fit freak
scarcely suits my wrecked physique.
This monument that's far more humble
's to the voice you're hearing grumble
that he's less on public view,
Heinrich Heine, poet and Jew.

Two grander monuments were planned
but turned down by the Fatherland,
though to the horror of the Habsburg court,
both had the Empress's support,
Elizabeth of Austria, Sissy, who
felt inspired by the soulful Jew
(but to be frank I wouldn't quote
the poems she claimed my spirit wrote!).
In 1892
Sissy took me to Corfu,
and statues Germany rejected
found safer spots to be erected
and with a more appealing view
of sea and cypress in Corfu
and, like many another hounded Jew,
the second statue found its way
to safe haven in the USA.

Your average Frankfurt-am-Mainer
doesn't give a shit for Heine
(nor, come to that, the young mainliner!).
So elbowed to one side back here,
surrounded by junked junkies' gear,
I, Heinrich Heine, have to gaze
on junkies winding tourniquets
made from the belt out of their jeans,
some scarcely older than their teens.
The Gorgon has them closely scanned
these new lost souls of ECU-land.

The Gorgon's glance gives them their high
then, trapped in her gaze, they petrify.

Schumann *lied*
(soprano)

Ach, meine Liebe selber
Zerfloß wie eitel Hauch!
Du alte, einsame Träne,
Zerfließe jetzunder auch!

Schumann set those words I wrote
that might bring lumps into your throat
(unless you grabbed for the remote!).
And even if you turned away
you could still hear the *lieder* play.
The marble Heine Deutschland banned
had this *lieder* in his hand,
a manuscript whose crumpled folds
a war-cracked index finger holds.
Where the statue goes the song goes too.
I took it with me to Corfu.
And wish to God I was still there
not here with bloodstains in my hair.
Europe's reluctant to shampoo
the gore-caked coiffure of the Jew,
the blood gushed from a botched injection,
in case it gives it some infection,
or maybe Europe doesn't care
there's junkies' blood in Heine's hair.

The gaze of modern Frankfurt's glued
to this glassy-eyed high altitude.
The Europe of the soaring cranes
has not seen fit to cleanse these stains
or give new hope to the stainer.

(soprano)

Was will die einsame Träne?

What is the music that redeems
desperate kids in such extremes?
Do those I hope you're watching need a
Schumann setting of my *lieder*?
'This lonely tear what doth it mean?'
we might well ask in such a scene.

Gaze and create. If art can't cope
it's just another form of dope,
and leaves the Gorgon in control
of all the freedoms of the soul.

[I can do nothing, even cry.
Tears are for the living eye.
So weep, you still alive to shed
the tears I can't shed, being dead.
And if I could I'd shed my tears
that in the century's closing years
the nations' greatest souls preside
over such spirit-suicide,
and that in 1992
Schiller, Goethe, Heine view
the new banks rising by the hour
above a park where chestnuts flower
whose canopies you'd think might cover
lunch-time lounger, reader, lover,
but for one who wrestles on his own
against the Gorgon who turns men to stone
the tree with white May blossom sways
like snakes that fringe the Gorgon's gaze,
the serpents that surround her stare.
Spring blossom hisses like her hair,
as this young junkie tries to choose
which vein today is best to use.]

Frankfurt police   The junkies' early evening high
is cut short by the *Polizei*,
who read the law they half-enforce,
and let some shoot-ups take their course.

The regular police routine
is shift the junkies in between
Schiller and Goethe every day
and pass by Heine on the way.

From Schiller's statue back to Goethe's
watching smartly dressed Frankfurters
enter the theatre, and dogs divide
the opiate from the Opera side.

The horns tune up, the dogs bark *'raus'*
the precincts of the opera house,
the maestro's rapturous ovations
kept safe by *Polizei* alsatians.
They glimpse a shoot-up then they go
for their own fix of *Figaro*,
see heroin addicts then go in
to hear heroes sing in *Lohengrin*,
and evening junkies grouped round Goethe
hear distorted *Zauberflöte*.
Music is so civilizing
for the place with new banks rising.
The main financial centre
of the EEC has to present a
fine *Turandot, Bohème, Cosí,*
for the European VIP.
Traviata, Faust, Aida,
even Schumann's setting of my *lieder,*
just to show, although it's mine,
I can put my own work on the line
and ask as the opera's about to start
what are we doing with our art?

Are we still strumming the right lyre
to play us through the century's fire?

['Bankfurt' they call it; by the way,
I was a banker in my day
and had a somewhat brief career
as Harry Heine banker here,
but the banks have grown and rather dwarf
the Jewish poet from Düsseldorf,
Not only me. Banks in the skies
cut even Goethe down to size.]

TONY HARRISON

With clouds of coins, cash cumuli
floating in the foyer sky
gliding guilder, hard ECU
dream clouds of 1992,
you'd think this Opera House foyer's
a long way from the Gorgon's gaze.
Escape, they're thinking, but alas
that's the Gorgon in the glass.

The ECU bank-erecting crane
reflected in van windowpane,
where, afraid of Aids, the youngsters queue
to trade old needles in for new,
though higher and higher into the blue
new banks to house the hard ECU
rise into the Frankfurt skies,
piece by piece, like Gorgon's eyes
or polished shield of one who slays
the Gorgon, but can't kill her gaze.

Schumann *lied*
(soprano)

Was will die einsame Träne?
Sie trübt mir ja den Blick.
Sie blieb aus alten Zeiten
In meinem Auge zurück.

Sie hatte viel leuchtende Schwestern,
Die alle zerfloßen sind.
Mit meinen Qualen und Freuden,
Zerfloßen in Nacht und Wind.

Wie Nebel sind auch zerflossen
Die blauen Sternelein,
Die mir jene Freuden und Qualen
Gelächelt ins Herz hinein.

Ach, meine Liebe selber
Zerfloß wie eitel Hauch!
Du alte, einsame Träne,
Zerfließe jetzunder auch!

Corfu shrine of
HEINRICH
HEINE

Isn't this a somewhat finer
monument to Heinrich Heine?
Banished from the Fatherland
with pen and *lieder* in my hand.
The *lieder* Schumann makes so touching
is in this manuscript I'm clutching,
and though war breaks round the manuscript
my hand will always keep it gripped.
But I'll have ten years of peace
with my Empress here in Greece
from this year 1892,
when Sissy brought me to Corfu.
[It was fun to have the Empress fawn
on one so much more lowly born
and so notorious a despiser
of King and Emperor and Kaiser,
those Krauts in crowns who used to squat
on Europe's thrones but now do not
wherever history's been rewritten,
that's everywhere but backward Britain,
but then I always found the English mind
compared to Europe's lagged behind.]

My shrine was in the forest glade
and up above she had displayed
Apollo with the lyre that plays
the darkness out of our dark days
in old times when Apollo's lyre
could save men from the petrifier.

For Sissy these weren't mere antiques,
these Muses of the ancient Greeks.
All the human spirit uses
to keep life's colour were the Muses,
or at least to Philhellenes like her
and many of her age they were.

[She retired from the Imperial Court
into art and poetry, music, thought,
though I really wouldn't care to quote
the poems she claimed my spirit wrote,

39

TONY HARRISON

most of her lines are deadly dull
but in all her soul is 'like a gull'
or 'swallow' like the ones that flew
around her Muses in Corfu
and though a palisade of peace
surrounded Sissy and myself in Greece
it was nonetheless a palisade
where Sissy thought and wrote and played.]

Music Room:
Schumann *lied*
(piano)

How would all these Muses fare
when dragged screaming by the hair
to gaze into the Gorgon's stare?

Dying Achilles
by Ernst Herter
(1884)

The fatal wound, the calf, the thigh
of Achilles who's about to die.
This hero of Homeric fame
gave Elizabeth's retreat its name.
This Achilles of 1884
foresees the future world of war
and shows the Empress half aware
of horrors brewing in the air.
Her presentiment and pity shows
in the Achilles that she chose,
helpless, unheroic, dying
watching clouds and seabirds flying
and not one so-called 'Eternal Being'
the Gorgon gulls us into seeing.
First the dead man's gaze goes rotten
then flies feast, then he's forgotten
after those who used to shed
their tears for him are also dead,
unless a bard like Homer brings
the dead redemption when he sings.
Along with me the Empress/versifier
revered blind Homer and his lyre

*Triumph of
Achilles* by Franz
Matsch

the ancient poet whose *Iliad*
was the steadiest gaze we'd ever had
at war and suffering Sissy thought
before the wars this century's fought.
Though melancholic, steeped in grief

the Gorgon was a mere motif
for Sissy who was unafraid
to have the Gorgon's face portrayed
on ironwork or balustrade,
and this almost charming Gorgon stares
from wardrobe doors and boudoir chairs,
but unwittingly they laid the track
that brought the grimmer Gorgon back

Schumann *lied*
(piano only)

[The palace style based on Pompeii's
might warn us of the Gorgon's gaze
but as her century drew to its close
still found poems in the rose,
the lily of loss and grieving hearts
until this closing century starts.]
The Empress posed above those roses
vanishes as her century closes
and the Muses she believed in threw
their roses to . . . I don't know who.
All the century's fresh bouquets
decayed beneath the Gorgon's gaze,
the grimmer Gorgon simply waited
till Sissy was assassinated
in the century's closing year,
which brought the German Kaiser here.
And when the Kaiser's gaze met mine
contemplating in my shrine,
the Kaiser's eye began to harden:
I don't want his kind in my garden.
He said straightaway: *Get rid
of Sissy's syphilitic Yid!*
Dammit! the man's a democrat
I've got no time for shits like that.
So once more the poet-refugee
was crated up and put to sea.
The crating up I had to face
the Kaiser wished on all my race.

And as the Kaiser wasn't keen
on Sissy's sentimental scene

of Achilles dying he'd make him stand
and represent the Fatherland.
He didn't like this sculpture much.
He liked his heroes much more butch,
more in his own imperious style.
He'd build an Achilles men could *heil*!

'Build my Achilles armour clad'
the Kaiser said, 'and confident in steel,
not some mama's little lad
with an arrow in his heel.

Make the wounded warrior stand
regrip his spear and gaze
through Sarajevo to the Fatherland,
the Lord of all that he surveys.

And put a Gorgon on his shield
to terrify his foes
wherever on Europe's battlefield

Triumphant
Achilles (statue)
by Johannes
Götz (1909)

the Kaiser's Gorgon goes?
And that is almost everywhere
as gazers freeze in stony sleep
seeing her eyes and coiling hair
hissing like chlorine gas at Ypres.

Doors opening.
Triumph of
Achilles
(painting)

The Kaiser, though a Homer freak,
despised the victim and the weak
and looking at Sissy's picture saw
Achilles riding high in war.
For him the focus of the painting
was triumph not some woman fainting,
but Sissy always used to see
Hector's wife, Andromache,
who has to gaze as Achilles hauls
her dead husband round Troy's walls.
The soon-to-be-defeated rows
of Trojans watch exultant foes
who bring the city to the ground
then leave it just a sandblown mound,
but the Greeks who'll watch Troy blaze

are also in the Gorgon's gaze,
the victims and the victimizer,
conquered and the conquering Kaiser,
Greeks and Trojans, Germans, Jews,
those who endure and those who use
the violence, that in different ways
keeps both beneath the Gorgon's gaze.
A whole culture vanished in the fire
until redeemed by Homer's lyre.
A lyre like Homer's could redeem
Hector's skull's still-echoing scream

Statue of
ACHILLES

Not like Sissy's Achilles sculpted dying
this one's triumphant, time defying.
The crane has hauled into the skies
the Kaiser in Homeric guise
(though not that you would recognize!)
Not only does this monster dwarf
the dissident from Düsseldorf
now newly banished from Corfu
it dwarfs all Sissy's Muses too.
What can lyre play or bard recite
the same scale as such armoured might
to face his gaze and still create?
Boxed up again inside a crate,
and forcibly reshipped
but still with pen and manuscript,
the shore receding, my last view
of my brief haven in Corfu,
hearing as cypresses recede a
fading phrase of my faint *lieder*,
was Achilles' spear whose gilded tip's
the Kaiser's signpost to Apocalypse.
Which of us, the marble Jew
the Kaiser kicked out of Corfu,
or armoured giant, him or me
would make it through the century?

TONY HARRISON

The founder of the 'master race'
put this inscription on its base.
Those cavities in secret braille
say: *All the Kaiser's work will fail!*
but, wrought in characters of weighty lead,
these pockmarks in the plinth once read:
'The greatest German to the greatest Greek.'
Though not quite equal in physique
the Kaiser's there in his creation,
emblem of his warlike nation,
this bellicose, Berlin-gazing totem
has hornets nesting in his scrotum.
Envenomed hordes have gone and built
their teeming nests in Prussia's kilt,
and perforate the scrotal sac
of the tutued 'Teutomaniac'.

Kaiser
excavation stills

But while all this trouble's brewing
what's the Prussian monarch doing?
We read in his own writing,
how, while all Europe geared for fighting,
England, Belgium, France and Russia
(but not of course his peaceful Prussia),
what was Kaiser Wilhelm II
up to? Excavating in Corfu,
the scholar Kaiser on the scent
of long lost temple pediment,
not filling trenches, excavating
the trenches where the Gorgon's waiting
there in the trench to supervise
the unearthing of the Gorgon's eyes.

This isn't how warmongers are,
this professor in a panama
stooping as the spades laid bare
the first glimpse of her snaky hair.

The excavator with his find,
a new art treasure for mankind.

The patient Kaiser, piece by piece,
prepares the Gorgon for release,
the Gorgon he let out to glower
above us all with baleful power.

Barbitos

The *barbitos*, the ancient lyre,
since the Kaiser's day,
is restrung with barbed wire.
Bards' hands bleed when they play
the score that fits an era's scream,
the blood, the suffering, the loss.
The twentieth-century theme
is played on barbed wire *barbitos*.

Terpsichore –
Achilleon

Terpsichore, the muse who sees
her dances done by amputees.
How can they hope to keep her beat
when war's destroyed their dancing feet?
Shelled at the Somme or gassed at Ypres,
they shuffle, hobble, limp and creep
and no matter what old air she plays
they can't escape the Gorgon's gaze.

Melpomene with
tragic mask

The tragic mask of ancient days
looked with eyes that never close
straight into the Gorgon's gaze
and sang Man's history through its throes.

But now where is she when we need her?
Tragedy's masks have changed their style.
Lips like these won't sing my *lieder*.
They've forgotten how to smile.

What poems will this mouth recite?
There'll be no Schumann sung from this.
Before these Germans went to fight
they'd been beautiful to kiss.

This is the Kaiser's Gorgon choir,
their petrifaction setting in,
grunting to the barbed-wire lyre,
gagging on snags of *Lohengrin*.

TONY HARRISON

Gorgon
pediment

With glaring eyes and hound-like snarls
from the maze-bound Meanderthals,
the Kaiser's Gorgon will preside
over ghettos, gulags, genocide.
Mankind meanders through the maze
made rigid by the Gorgon's gaze.
Following a more flowing shape
might find us freedom and escape
from the Gorgon and her excavator
who gears his kind for horrors later.
The Kaiser couldn't stand one Jew
in marble near him in Corfu
but the Kaiser's not uncommon views
were just as vicious on all Jews:
'A poison fungus on the German oak'
(to quote the bastard makes me choke!)
This is how the Gorgon blinds
her henchmen's eyes and rigid minds.

Arrow motif on
pediment

The Gorgon worshippers unroll
the barbed wire gulags round the soul.
The Gorgon's henchmen try to force
History on a straighter course
with Gorgonisms that impose
fixities on all that flows,
with Führer fix and crucifix
and Freedom-freezing politics.
Each leader on his monstrous plinth
waves us back into the labyrinth
out of the meander and the maze
straight back into the Gorgon's gaze.

Gorgon motif
into swastika

The Kaiser in his notebook drew
where the Gorgon leads us to,
step by step and stage by stage
he steers the Gorgon through our age.
Her hand on his unlocks the door
that never will quite close on War.

46

The junkie and the nationalist
both get their fixes with clenched fist.
And even in the ECU-world
the Kaiser's flag's once more unfurled.

Ocean-borne
bodies and Nazi
flag

My statue, meanwhile, got away
with swastikas daubed on my face
out of Hamburg to Marseilles
to Toulon and a new safe base.

And apart from finger, nose and pen
my statue's pretty much intact
but those that let the Gorgon out on men
are totally broken and cracked.

Statues of
Gorgon's
henchmen being
demolished

HEINE's statue
in Toulon

My statue, meanwhile, got away
with swastikas daubed on my face
out of Hamburg to Marseilles
to Toulon and a new safe base.

And apart from finger, nose and pen
my statue's pretty much intact,
but those that let the Gorgon out on men
are totally broken and cracked.

Banished from the Fatherland
still with my *lieder* in my hand
though the pen the poems flowed from
was shattered by an air-raid bomb,
so being without it I recite
as I do now what I can't write.
The *lieder* Schumann makes so touching
is in the manuscript I'm clutching.
This manuscript with faded writing
survived a century of fighting.
Though war broke round this manuscript
my broken hand has kept it gripped.

Toulon *lied*,
Schumann arr.
Kiszko

[No longer hunted or hounded
and safe and far from fear.
If all the dogs are silenced
why do my eyes shed this tear?

47

The tears I let fall on the journey
were falling for all I saw.
Today I gaze on the ocean
so far from the fear of war.

The gloom that surrounds those frozen
beneath the Gorgon's gaze
now falls as the century's shadow
to darken our hearts and days.

And though I gaze in sunlight
on springtime's brightest hues,
no longer hunted and hounded,
(End *lied*)   I weep for six million Jews.]

But when through dappled shades of green
I catch glimpses of a submarine,
and across the ocean have to face
through waving palms a naval base,
it's then I'm reassured to know
that just a hundred years ago
when this rejected marble Jew
escaped with Sissy to Corfu
my other monument made its way
to safe haven in the USA,
safe from Europe's old alarms
into the New World Order's arms.

The Bronx, New   The Gorgon who's been running riot
York   through the century now seems quiet,
but supposing one who's watched her ways
were to warn you that the Gorgon's gaze
remains unburied in your day
and I've glimpsed her even in the USA,
you'll all reply he's crying wolf,
Gulf War   but in the deserts of the Gulf
steel pediments have Gorgon's eyes
now grown as big as tank-wheel size
that gaze down from her temple frieze
on all her rigid devotees.

Skull – *lied*,
Schumann arr.
Kiszko (soprano)

The closing century's shadow
has darkened all our years
and still the Gorgon's filling
my empty sockets with tears.

The tears I let fall in the desert
the sand has all soaked away.
My eyes and all that they gazed on
are gone from the light of day.

They've gone with these palls of blackness
the smoking desert blaze.
Will all of our freedoms and glories
end up in the Gorgon's gaze?

O so much life has vanished
in smoking fiery skies.
The closing century's shadow

(end *lied*)

is cast across all our eyes.

*Triumph of
Achilles* (detail)

The empty helmet of one whose eyes
have gone to feast the desert flies,
the eyes of one whose fate was sealed
by Operation Desert Shield.
They gazed their last these dark dark sockets
on high-tech Coalition rockets.

Tourists

Soon, in 1994,
in this palace Greece starts to restore,
in this the Kaiser's old retreat
Europe's heads of state will meet,
as the continent disintegrates
once more into the separate states
that waved their little flags and warred
when the Kaiser's Gorgon was abroad.
So to commemorate that rendezvous
of ECU statesmen in Corfu
I propose that in that year
they bring the dissident back here,
and to keep new Europe open-eyed

Painter in the
Achilleon singing

they let the marble poet preside . . .

49

THE BLASPHEMERS' BANQUET

The Blasphemers' Banquet was first broadcast on BBC1
on 31 July 1989.

Music Dominic Muldowney
Sung by Teresa Stratas

The Misanthrope of Molière (trans. Tony Harrison) Edward Pether-
bridge as Philinte, David Horovitch as Alceste, and Donald Pickering
as Oronte

Voltaire's Follies (Paris) with Jean François Prevand, Gerard Maro,
Yves Pignot and Remy Kirch

Voice of Rev. Wallace Brian Cox

Photography Mike Fox, Paola Ribeiro
Sound Recordist Fraser Barber
Additional Photography Colin Clarke
Additional Sound David Keene
Dubbing Mixer Stuart Grieg
Special Sound Andrew Wilson
Dubbing Editor Stuart Napier
Video-tape Editor Peter Belcher
Designer Edward Lipscombe
Graphic Designer Andrew Hunter
Production Secretary Teresa Watts
Production Assistant Sally Corfield
Researchers Harriet Bakewell, Amanda Barrett
Film Editor Peter Simpson
Executive Producer David Pearson
Director Peter Symes

The blasphemers' banquet table: there
on mirrored cushions will sit Voltaire,
me, Molière, Omar Khayyam, Lord Byron
and that, that's Salman Rushdie's chair.

It's perfect for tonight's blasphemers' meeting,
this place renowned in Bradford for good eating
that used to be a church and gets its name
from the poet who loves *this* life, however fleeting,

Omar Khayyam, who also loved his wine and had no care
for those cascade-crammed castles in the air
the Koran promises to those who sacrifice
'this fleeting life' for afterlife up there.

Often called the 'Voltaire of the East',
Omar Khayyam will pour wine at our feast
and I'll propose the toast to Salman Rushdie
and all those, then or now, damned by some priest.

'And frankly I wish I'd written a more critical book.'

'Kill the bastard, burn him . . . kill the bastard . . . burn him to death.'

When I see bigots wanting Rushdie dead
burning a book I'm sure they've never read,
marble bust or not, Voltaire's got stored
a much more critical book in this old head.

I too heard bigots rant, rave and revile
books of mine which, after a short while
were canonized as classics, which is why
you always see Voltaire with this wry smile.

A boy in Abbeville for having sung
a mildly blasphemous ballad had his tongue
ripped from its roots, and on his blazing body
my *Philosophical Dictionary* was flung.

53

TONY HARRISON

And I whose books got flung into the blaze
of Inquisitorial *auto da fés*

Comédie
Française foyer

am now a monument with Molière
in the Crush Bar of the Comédie Française.

Voltaire's statue
reflected in TV
monitor
dissolves to
reveal funeral of
Ayatollah
Khomeini

[Superimposed quotation, Ayatollah Khomeini]
*'I know that during my long life I have always been right about
what I said.'*

TERESA
STRATAS (sung
refrain)

'Oh, I love this fleeting life.'

The Koran denounces unbelievers who
quote 'love this fleeting life' unquote. I do.
I'm an unbeliever. I love this life.
I don't believe their paradise is true.

Sparkling water
(Bradford
fountain near
site of book
burning)

The afterlife for which that chilled corpse prayed
was a paradise of fountains and green shade
and dark-eyed houris and a garden
where roses bloom forever and don't fade

unlike this world of ours where things fade fast.
In a place where nothing changes and things last
the *fatwa* Fascist lolls in Paradise
and waters full of stars go flowing past.

[Superimposed quotation, Ayatollah Khomeini]
*'These are things which are impure: urine, excrement, sperm,
blood, dogs, pigs, unbelievers, wine, beer and the sweat of the
excrement-eating camel.'*

And as a righteous man he'll be arrayed
in richest silks and delicate brocade
and be served sherbets by chaste virgins,
he, whose *fatwa* made the world afraid.

54

And while the Ayatollah, at a fountain's side
chooses some dark-eyed virgin for a bride,
down here where life is fleeting and time flies
a man I've asked to dinner has to hide.

TONY
HARRISON
sitting in
Bradford square

This isn't paradise but the Bradford square
where Rushdie's book got burnt, just over there.
By reading it, where fools had it cremated
I bring it whole again, out of the air.

*The Satanic
Verses* appears
out of thin air
and into his
hands

Near where the National Theatre does a play
by one priests smeared as Satan in his day
I read a book by one dubbed Satan now
whose work, like Molière's, is here to stay.

And of the afterlife I have no heed.
What more could a godless mortal need
than a samosa and a can of beer
and books, like Rushdie's, to sit here and read?

Crane shot,
Bradford city
centre

And I've asked its hidden author out to eat
with five blasphemers he might like to meet
at the OMAR KHAYYAM Tandoori
not far from here near Bradford's Paradise Street.

At this blasphemers' banquet I've set up
Omar Khayyam will cry 'Come Fill the Cup'
and Molière, Voltaire, Lord Byron and myself
will toast *The Satanic Verses* when we sup.

Omar Khayyam, the poet of Iran
whose quatrain I'm using here, as best I can,
will pour for us his choicest flask of wine
while I pass round the Peshawari nan.

Queen Victoria
statue, Bradford;
statue and
Alhambra
Theatre

Blasphemers sharing Bradford bread and wine
are due to rendezvous at half past nine
after blasphemer Molière at the Alhambra
in a blasphemer's English version – mine.

PHILINTE

*'Your black philosophy's too bleak by half.
Your moods of black despair just make me laugh
I think by now I know you pretty well . . .*

We're very like Ariste and Sganerelle,
the brothers in that thing by Molière,
You know, 'The School of Husbands', that one where . . .'

ALCESTE 'For God's sake, spare us Molière quotations.

[Superimposed quotation, Ayatollah Khomeini]
'There is no humour . . . in Islam
There is no laughter . . . in Islam
There is no fun . . . in Islam'

ORONTE '. . . but still I'm at a loss to know what's in my poem.'

ALCESTE 'Jesus wept! It's bloody rubbish . . .'

Int. theatre

Priests may turn to piety and prayer,
I turn to poetry and plays by Molière.
'Theatre', said Hugo, 'is a place for forming souls',
but the only gods it knows are those up there.

Theatre lights
fading

Believing only in this life below,
these are the only gods I'll ever know.
We live and die and only time destroys us,
falling forever into the big 'O'.

That great big O of nothingness that swallows
poets and priests, queens and Ayatollahs
not only infidels but fundamentalists
whether in black turbans or dog collars.

Molière burst in
Comédie
Française

In Molière's own time these pious frauds
thought it a blasphemy to tread the boards.
He'd be gratified to see his 'blasphemies'
doing slightly better business than the 'Lord's'.

Int. theatre:
lights fade out

Because he died and no priest heard him swear
that he abjured the stage, this Molière
was buried without candles at the dead of night
a fate the Church made many actors share.

Sung refrain: 'We live and die and only time destroys us.'

Charles Rice's
tomb,
Undercliffe
cemetery,
Bradford

Bradford, when Charles Rice was alive,
saw the Church and theatres both thrive;
now the churches have new uses and of the theatres
only the Alhambra managed to survive.

Track from
tombs to wide
shot Bradford

And of the many churches Charles Rice knew
of those left standing there are very few
with singing Sabbath congregations; mosques
are the only sacred houses now built new.

One church where some of these at rest come from's
long since flattened by Luftwaffe bombs,
the Four Square Gospel Church is auction rooms,
the Presbyterian purveys crisp popadums.

The golden dome and muezzin's minaret
as panoramas on his panto set
for *Ali Baba* or *Aladdin* at the Royal
were all the Orient that Charles Rice met.

Gravestone with
Omar Khayyam
quotation

The only influence then out of Iran
before the fanatic Ayatollah, was a man
who praised wine and despised the Paradise
promised to Moslem *men* by the Koran.

But this Bradford tomb with Rubai'yat quatrain
faces the half-built mosque in East Squire Lane,
its gold dome shining, and so new
it's still not felt a drop of Bradford rain.

Still domeless girders open to the sky,
an even bigger mosque goes up nearby,
our church/tandoori rendezvous, named after
the poet who penned this gravestone's gold *rubai*:

'*Lo some we loved the loveliest and the best
that time and fate of all their vintage pressed
have drunk their cup a round or two before
and one by one crept silently to rest.*'

Sung refrain

'*Oh*'

TONY HARRISON

Camera moves
from graveyard
down to
restaurant/
church

'*Oh, I love this fleeting life.*'

'*Oh*'

'*Omar Khayyam*'

REV.
ALEXANDER
WALLACE
(quoted from
sermon of 1853)

'*Oh, that I could but rightly speak of the practical influence
which the life of Christ ought to exert upon us all. He went
about doing good that he might influence us to do the same.*'

Int. restaurant

St Andrews built in 1849
nourishes Bradford under a new sign
and beer and Bombay special biryani
oust Bible bombast from the Scots divine.

And imbibers have a few months' grace before
these girders get their gold dome on next door
and muezzin's call sours Omar's ruby vintage
curdling the stomach of the currievore.

Where there was passionate preaching and packed pews
are King Prawn Rogan Josh and Vindaloos.
For Bradford devotees of Indian food
the OMAR KHAYYAM restaurant is 'good news'.

The blasphemers' banquet table, there
on mirrored cushions will sit Voltaire,
me, Molière, Omar Khayyam, Lord Byron
and that, that's Salman Rushdie's chair.

REV. WALLACE

'*A wine bibber, oh that we could imbibe that spirit, oh
surely . . .*'

Ruined or
altered Bradford
churches

They sing of time that bears us all away
and how God alone's resistant to decay.
But his congregations and his churches aren't;
where's the pulpit, where's the cross, and where are
they?

58

Abandoned
graveyard

Where some of Bradford's past already lies
life flowers in these bright affirming eyes,
though her forehead rests on some old grave
she thinks that time stays still, and never flies.

It won't be long before she knows
that everything will vanish with the rose
and then she'll either love life more because it's fleeting
or hate the flower and life because it goes.

Indian children

Beautiful sisters in their white and green
innocent of what these crude words mean
but maybe they will soon discover beauty

Track from
obscene graffiti
on wall to new
mosque

is inescapably bound up with the obscene.

Graffiti:
'Scarface
bumbed his Dad
upside down. he
licked his mum
Fanny out 200
Time a minute'

Various creeds attempt to but can't split
the world of spirit from the world of shit.
Crude scrawls and sacred scrolls come from one
      mind.
Scarface subverts the saint and won't submit.

This message LEAVE NO LITTER in Urdu
seems to have some problem getting through.
Man's fear of his own filth makes him go seeking
the unblemished beautiful in the untrue.

The thorny whys and wherefores, awkward whences,
things that seduce or shame or shock the senses
panic the one-book creeds into erecting
a fence against all filth and all offences.

Feeling that life seems blasted by some blight
we keep on yearning for some purer light

Undercliffe
cemetery, tomb
– move down to
auction rooms in
town

but this, as Bertrand Russell wrote, is born
from our deep fear of everlasting night,

fear of that big O that swallows whole
both the human body and the soul,
fear of time that makes us live and die,
fear of transience that takes its daily toll,

Southend Hall Auction Rooms	fear of living, fear of being dead, fear that what we love most's soonest fled, fear of loving what is fleeting for itself our fear of what false prophets make us dread,

of doomsday with its dreadful but false dooms,
of time that bustles men back into tombs,

Int. auction rooms

of that fleeting transience that can transform
the Four Square Gospel Church to auction rooms,

the transience that makes the life-warmed ring
dangle for buyers from a numbered string
and numbers us, knick-knacks of nothingness,
the going – going – gone of everything.

DAVID BISHOP
(auctioneer)

*'Start me at a pound for the lot, I've a pound, two, have we two
now, have we one, are we done now? Couldn't you take
something at fifty quid? Who was it? Mrs Bennett.*
One five four. One five four is the gold ring. One five four.
Where shall we have a tenner, a fiver then. A gold ring is this.
Must be at scrap value at this sort of money. Start me at a fiver.
*Three pounds then. Have we three? Right we haven't. Put it
down Brian.*
*Silver frame, one five five. One five five, the silver frame. Forty
pounds for it . . . twenty then . . .'*

Bishops once burned books (and people!), here
it's Mr Bishop, Bradford auctioneer
who has them boxed and bundled in job lots
with wedding rings and repro jardinière.

Sung refrain

'Oh I love this fleeting life.'

Camera pans
across room and
television sets

*'Thirty-five, now, you can't beat tuning into the mass media,
fount of all knowledge is that. Are we all done at thirty-five
pounds then? Is that it? And it's Mr Capstick at thirty-five
pounds.*
*Lot two six seven are three bundles of books. Many tomes of
ancient knowledge there. Here we go. Where shall it be, at
twenty pounds, I've a tenner, a fiver, only bid at seven. Tenner
you're trying, twelve, at fourteen now, at fourteen, sixteen,
eighteen, are we done at sixteen?*

Marble bust of
Voltaire

*All right, we've two fifty three now which is . . . what is it made
of? Marble? It's marble isn't it Brian? This marble bust. Right*

*two fifty three, where do we start this? Unusual item, quickly
then . . . sixteen, eighteen, twenty, I've twenty bid. Are we all
done at twenty pounds? Mr Nicholson at twenty pounds,
Harrison at twenty pounds. Well, there's one thing that can be
said, your fame's not travelled before you, is that correct sir?
Thank you. Right . . .'*

TONY
HARRISON

Time, that gives and takes our fame and fate
and puts say, Shakespeare's features on a plate
or a Persian poet's name on a Tandoori
can cast aside all we commemorate

and make Lot 86 or Lot 14
even out of Cardinal and Queen

HM Queen on
biscuit tin

and bring the holy and the high and mighty
to the falling gavel, or the guillotine.

Voltaire bust
Paris: Place de la
République
(news footage
and actuality)

When a small boy bellows *Mort! Mort! Mort!*
for Salman Rushdie and fanatics roar
Death to the imagination a revival's due
of work I wrote two centuries before.

When I have to watch this Paris square
packed with murderous protest, then with prayer

London
demonstration
against Rushdie
27 May 1989

at the feet of the Republic then it's time
that France (and even Britain) read Voltaire.

Sung refrain

*'Oh, I love this fleeting life
Oh, I love this fleeting life'*

War memorial

Byron statue in
Hyde Park

Lord Byron heaves a bronze Byronic sigh
to see familiar bigotry march by
but being dead since 1824
and cast in bronze he casts a colder eye.

Robert Southey, Poet Laureate and fool
said Byron headed the 'Satanic School'
of poetry, which, he thundered, undermined
all religious faith and moral rule,

61

TONY HARRISON

Byron cartoon	and a Satanic poet, so Southey said, goes on accumulating guilt when he is dead as long as copies of his verses circulate and go on, unlike Southey's, being read.
Statue	My Satanic poems, Satanic play made bigots brand me Satan in my day. Have patience, brother Satan, you might be a bronze, like me, in Bradford or Bombay.
Crowd	*'Kill the bastard . . .'*

And down the river, just a little way
the National Theatre's done a matinée
of a 300-year-old piece by Molière

Paris fountain — branded by bigots the Satan of his day.

And those condemned in God's or Allah's name

Comédie Française; Molière statue; Voltaire statue — may end up statues in the Hall of Fame.
'The most irreligious man who ever lived'
some priest called Molière. *I* got the same.

Molière's *Tartuffe* the first French play
to strip hypocrisy's sour mask away
was the one most hated by fundamentalists
till my play about the prophet: MAHOMET.

Seq. from 'Mahomet' — *'Allah, Allah, Allah . . .'*

Play develops into extended sequence of fundamentalist religions — Though not much played since 1742
a revival of my play's long overdue.
By MAHOMET I meant all fundamentalists
Moslem, Catholic, Protestant and Jew.

REV. IAN PAISLEY — *'We have to preserve and maintain in this island True Protestantism, and the Protestant way of life. And I have news for the Roman Catholic church in Ireland today, we Protestants are here in Ireland to stay.'*

RABBI MEIR
KAHANE

'. . . *you know someone who wants to, who wants to kill you*
. . . get up first and go and kill him first, that is Judaism, that is
Judaism, that is sanity.'

MOTHER
ANGELICA

'*It is without question the most blasphemous, the most*
disrespectful, the most satanic movie that's ever been made . . .'

[Image of Ayatollah Khomeini]

US PREACHER

'. . . *the world passeth away*'

[Seq. ends on bleeding boy and fountain in Hyde Park at end of
demonstration]

Sung refrain

'*Oh, I love this fleeting life . . .*'
Oh, I love this fleeting life . . .'

Restaurant

There's me, and one-two-three-four-five!
Four of them can't come, they're not alive
and one who can't because the *fatwa* Führer
forced him into hiding to survive.

Right from the beginning I'm afraid I knew
you'd never make our Bradford rendezvous.
But my invitation was a way of showing
things you still might like to but *can't* do,

say, stroll round Bradford like I did today,
watch the Comédie Française perform a play,
a child pilot a chopper on a roundabout,
applaud the Voltaire Follies' MAHOMET.

The Ayatollah forced you to decline
my invitation to share food and wine
with poets branded as blasphemers
including Omar, now our restaurant sign.

Omar Khayyam, the poet of Iran
the 'Voltaire of Persia' and a man
who praised wine, and despised the Paradise
promised to Moslem *men* by the Koran.

*The Ayatollah in his rich brocades
sucking sherbets by shimmering cascades
nods approval to the theologian
who wants the world to kill all those with Aids.

*Note the new name: Abdullah-al-Mashad,
the latest mullah, dangerous and mad —
'Frankly, I wish I'd written a more critical book' —
Sadly, Salman, I sometimes wish you had!

SALMAN
RUSHDIE

The dead don't dine, those under threat
are not at liberty to come here yet.
But when you're free you're welcome and meanwhile
I toast your talent on your TV set.

Where you're in hiding, tuned to the BBC,
I hope you get some joy in watching me
raise my glass to *The Satanic Verses*,
to its brilliance and, yes, its blasphemy.

Its blasphemy enabled man
to break free from the Bible and Koran
with their life-denying fundamentalists
and hell-fire such fanatics love to fan.

Omar loves 'this fleeting life' and knows
that everything will vanish with the rose
and yet, instead of Paradise prefers
this life of passion, pain and passing shows.

Omar writes how nothing stays the same
and it's an irony of fleeting fame
that this Tandoori, OMAR KHAYYAM today

Ext. restaurant.   tomorrow will be called another name.

[Sung refrain of the letters coming down as the workers
dismantle the restaurant sign.]

* Under legal pressure the BBC removed these two quatrains from the film, though the
Independent had published a Reuters report from Sara-el-Gammal quoting the head of
the Fatwa Committee of Al-Azhar University.

LOVING MEMORY
The Muffled Bells
Mimmo Perrella non è Piu
Cheating the Void
Letters in the Rock

Loving Memory, a series of four film / poems written and presented by Tony Harrison and produced by Peter Symes, was first broadcast on BBC2 in July and August 1987.

The Muffled Bells was first broadcast on 30 July 1987.

Cameraman Steve Saunderson
Sound Recordist Trevor Gosling
Dubbing Mixer Alan Dykes
Lighting Electrician Alex Scott
Grips Alan Imeson
Graphics Paul Johnson
Production Assistant Lisbet Heath
Research Florence Minnis
Film Editor Peter Simpson

Mimmo Perrella non è Piu was first broadcast on 23 July 1987.

Photography John Goodyer, Graham Frake
Sound Recordist Roger Long
Dubbing Mixer Alan Dykes
Production Assistant Lisbet Heath
Researcher Tiziana Toglia
Film Editor Liz Thoyts
Producer Michael Hutchinson

Cheating the Void was first broadcast on 6 August 1987.

Photography Brian Hall, Steve Saunderson
Sound Recordists Roger Long, Trevor Gosling
Dubbing Mixer Alan Dykes
Lighting Electrician Dusty Miller
Grips Alan Imeson
Production Assistants Lisbet Heath, Catherine Barnes
Assistant Producer Michael Hutchinson
Associate Producer Colin Rose
Film Editor Peter Simpson

Letters in the Rock was first broadcast on 16 July 1987.

Cameramen Steve Saunderson, Paul Morris
Sound Recordists Trevor Gosling, Lyndon Bird
Dubbing Mixer Alan Dykes
Lighting Electrician Alex Scott
Grips Alan Imeson
Graphics Paul Johnson
Research Florence Minnis, Nick Shearman
Production Assistant Lisbet Heath
Assistant Producer Michael Hutchinson
Associate Producer Colin Rose
Film Editor Peter Simpson

The Muffled Bells

Int. church: muffles being put on bells

They're muffling the bells for Stanley Hall.
Stanley Hall the Breamore miller's dead.
Clappers in cowhide cladding peel and call
all those who used his flour in their bread.

Farmer with geese

He hears the curfew toll for Stanley Hall,
Ed Trim seen fattening his Christmas geese
will be one of four friends who bear his pall
when the Breamore miller goes to rest in peace.

Horses ploughing, cows standing in water, etc.

Muffled curfew, flock of geese, the plough,
some things survive from 'how things used to be',
though much is vanishing and threatened now
Breamore's bells are pure Gray's *Elegy*.

'The Curfew tolls the Knell of parting Day,
The lowing Herd winds slowly o'er the Lea,
The Plow-man homeward plods his weary Way,
And leaves the World to Darkness, and to me.

Now fades the glimmering Landscape on the Sight,
And all the Air a solemn Stillness holds;
Save where the Beetle wheels his droning Flight,
And drowsy Tinklings lull the distant Folds.

Beneath those rugged Elms, that Yew-Tree's Shade,
Where heaves the Turf in many a mould'ring Heap,
Each in his narrow Cell for ever laid,
The rude Forefathers of the Hamlet sleep.

Far from the Madding Crowd's ignoble Strife,
Their sober Wishes never learn'd to stray;
Along the cool sequester'd Vale of Life
They kept the noiseless Tenor of their Way.

Yet ev'n these Bones from Insult to protect
Some frail Memorial still erected nigh,
With uncouth Rhimes and shapeless Sculpture deck'd,
Implores the passing Tribute of a Sigh.

TONY HARRISON

Their Name, their Years, spelt by th'unlettered
                                          Muse,
The Place of Fame and Elegy supply:
And many a holy Text around she strews,
That teach the rustic Moralist to dye.'

A lichened quatrain chiselled in the year
1750 when the poet Gray
first wrote the Elegy I'm reading here,
this rustic moralist what does he say?

Tombstone   *'Come hither mortal, cast an eye*
then go thy way prepared to die.
Twill be thy doom to know thou must
like me at last be turned to dust.'

Strange how poetry most people think a bore,
poetry that people of our period despise
or if they don't despise it just ignore,
seems to surface fast when someone dies.

Tombstone   *'I was but young and in my bloom*
My morning sun was set at noon
Grieve not for me my glass is full
It is the Lord his will.'

Craftsmen, wheelwright, blacksmith, undertaker,
who also turned a skilled hand to the plough
gathered in harvests grateful to their Maker
are in decline, as Gray's own craft is, now.

Now that the village's last miller's dead
his craft of milling flour has also died.
Flour from Breamore fields went into bread
that's been replaced by pre-sliced *Mother's Pride*.

Breamore village   The new commuters eye the empty mill,
the sequestered vale's a teeming motorway.
But in spite of creeping yuppies Breamore's still
the sort of churchyard known to Thomas Gray.

Though the curfew's being tolled for the old ways
and the mill and manor are developers' desires
Breamore's going to stay the way it stays
while it's Sir Westrow Hulse, the present squire's.

Vicar with Sir
Westrow and
Lady Hulse by
church door

'Morning to you. I gather it was all a great success yesterday, did
it go well?'

The squire who owns Stan's mill and all the land
that gives Harvests that they've come to thank God for.
He pays the rector who's just shook his hand.
He enters the Saxon church by his own door.

Breamore remembers in its autumn prayers
and memories are in Sir Westrow's head
for those who lie outside in seven layers
the village's long roll-call of the dead.

Norman Dymott, sexton, rings the bell
for families of men who marched away
in World War One and those of them who fell

Roll of Honour

are marked on the Roll of Honour with a K.

Two congregations: one, in seven layers,
stays silent as the other sings the hymns,
the Vinces and the Walkers and the Wares,
the Witts, the Dymotts and the Trims.

Int. church:
congregation
stands

'Come ye thankful people come,
Raise the song of harvest-home:
All is safely gathered in,
Ere the winter storms begin;
God, our Maker, doth provide
For our wants to be . . .'

The choir consists of thirty generations
though most of them are muffled underground.
The minority, this present congregation's
singing for the dead who lie all round.

TONY HARRISON

'... the song of harvest-home.
All this world is God's own field,
Fruit unto his praise to yield ...'

The man who'll dig the grave for Stanley Hall,
thrusting his sexton's spade in with his boot,
is the same who gave the bell's unmuffled call
to Breamore's blessing of its flowers and fruit.

'Ripening with a wondrous power
Till the final harvest-hour:
Grant, O Lord of life, that we
Holy grain and pure may be.'

Norman Dymott (sexton)

'The majority of the people that's buried here are parishioners and you've lived with them, and been brought up with them and therefore you know there's a personal touch in them, and it's a lovely feeling that you can still walk back into your old village church and churchyard and find that your old relatives and workmates are still there with you.'

Marking out grave

'The first thing sort of with any funeral, I get a phone call from the undertaker and he gives me the person concerned, the size of the grave, the time of the funeral and from then on we, you know, make preparation for digging the grave.'

'My father he actually took over from William Nicklin that lived in the cottage near the church, he got killed in the 1914–18 War and father was then pleaded out of the Army and he took over from him, and it's just carried on, I helped him when I was old enough and when father died I took over from father and we're today carrying on, with the help of John, my friend here to do the donkey work.'

They're measuring the ground for Stanley Hall.
They don't need to know what Stan's statistics are,
they were his neighbours and they know how tall
the man was they stood next to at the bar.

Coffin-making

John Shering gives hard elm a final shave
to demonstrate another dying trade,
most people these days go into the grave
in a coffin of veneer that's factory-made.

The grooves a carpenter bends coffins by
he calls the *curfs*, a local Hampshire word
that, like what it describes, will also die
and, like the Breamore miller, be interred.

JOHN SHERING
(undertaker)

'I've been undertaking for forty years and the family have been
undertakers for the last 200 years. All the Sherings, all that time
have all been carpenters and the village carpenter was the
undertaker.'

'Coffins aren't like this very often now, this is too hard work for
us all. The fresh method is they're made in factories with
machines that cut each board, they mitre the corners, they use
machines to tack them together, they're a lot lighter. This
method is the method that has been used for hundreds of years
and when I started we always made coffins just like this. This is
elm that was cut down after it was caught with Dutch elm
disease. Cut down about a mile away from here, and sawn up,
and we've kept this wood for ten years, and it's got good and
hard now. Hard to work. We've still got some more board if
anybody needs one.'

NORMAN
DYMOTT

'When you chat about coffins these days they're nearly all
veneered to what they were solid oak or elm in the days gone by.
To prove how long an oak coffin will last against a veneered one,
in the corner of the churchyard there I've exhumed a body that
had been there for twenty-five years and that coffin was still
absolutely intact and solid and the lid and everything was
absolutely solid still. Admitted it was in gravel soil that was you
know was draining, good drainage, but goes to prove the
difference between a veneer coffin and a solid oak coffin. The
veneered coffin I should say you could give it twelve months and
the lid's caved in, specially in wet heavy soil, there's a vast
difference in the lasting power and also the price.'

JOHN SHERING

'And my father and I used to carry a coffin out at dusk, 'cause
most people stayed in their houses in those days, and we would
carry a coffin at dusk on our shoulders through the town, and
really nobody took a lot of notice of us. I don't know what
would happen now if someone was seen carrying a coffin
through the town at dusk, but everything seemed normal then.'

'Being an undertaker isn't just dealing with the coffin and the one
who has died. The most important people we look to are the
relatives because we do everything for them, we undertake to do
everything for them, even if it's just talking, or even if it's not
just talking, but sitting and maybe holding their hands. I think
it's important that you talk about the person who has died, just

73

TONY HARRISON

because they've died and may be been buried or cremated they're
still people in people's memories and you should talk about
them.'

John buries people but exhumes the past.
His museum helps the village to recall
with village things and photos he's amassed,
like maybe the miller's tools of Stanley Hall.

Brass plates in
museum

Off solid oak and elm these coffin plates
from the layer before the one where Stan will lie
are all that's left of those who met their fates
in what Norman Dymott calls 'the days gone by'.

Children
rehearsing
Annie, singing

'It's a hard knock life
Got no folks to speak of so
It's the hard-knock row we hoe . . .'

JOHN SHERING

'The museum is used for lots of things. The choral society use it
for a sort of practice room. We rehearse plays in there.'

Children singing

'Don't it feel like the wind is always howling,
Don't it seem like there's never any light?
Once a day, don't you wanna throw the towel in?
It's easier than puttin' up a fight.'

'No one's there when your dreams at night get creepy,
No one cares if you grow . . . or if you shrink
No one dries when your eyes get . . .'

JOHN SHERING

'These funeral cards are collected over the
years and people hand them in. They were
sent out as mourning cards, not used now.'

Children singing

'. . . running free in NYC
Bet she finds her folk
Like that
Mom and Dad
Right off the bat
Lucky duck, she got away
But we're gonna have to pay
Gonna get our faces slapped
Gonna get our knuckles rapped
It's a hard knock life
Yes it is
It's a hard knock life . . .'

Maybe Stanley Hall made this girl weep –

74

Children singing	'. . . yes it is It's a hard knock life . . .'

Maybe Stanley Hall pulled these girls' hair —

Children singing	'. . . it's a hard knock life — Yes it is!'

Most and not maybe are now six feet deep,
forming the country churchyard's seventh layer.

Tombstone	Catherine Sarah Taunton, 33, who passed away in 1859 a century too late for *Gray*'s elegy but at least still legible enough for mine.

Tombstone	*'A wife so kind a friend sincere* *A tender mother lieth here* *We weep on earth in vain* *But in Heaven we hope to meet again.* *Here then in hope of endless life* *Rest three children and a wife.'*

Damaged stones with names of Snow, Frost, Dew	Not many tombs survive from Gray's own day, gravestones afforded only by the few after their occupants themselves decay, worn down by Hampshire rain, Snow, Frost and Dew.

Who were also Breamore rectors whose remains
are appropriately close together
but none, though in his element, sustains
the pressure of their eponyms of weather.

TONY LIGHT	*'Gravestones were an important aspect of historical research, but* *as with memories of the more recent families in the village, their* *use is fairly limited, and we really need to use the historical* *documents which survive to build up a proper picture, a more* *complete picture of many of the families, and I've been* *cataloguing the documents up at the House here for the past ten* *years or so.'*

'My, I think it was great-great-grandfather came to Breamore as coachman to the family at the house here in about 1860 and they've been resident in Breamore ever since.'

'Only one gravestone survives from before 1700, and even for the past two centuries probably no more than one in six of the villagers ever had their own memorials erected because of the cost.'

'The very richest and the highest actually laid claim to a place in the church itself for burial and the aim was always to get as near to the door of the church as possible if you couldn't actually afford to get inside, and as we go further away from the church itself the number of box tombs actually becomes very small generally and there's a general mixture of dates and types of tombs and all classes of people, except the very poorest of course who aren't actually commemorated.'

Unmarked grave
(mound)

'Until relatively recently most villages were virtually self-sufficient in the basic crafts and many of the gravestones actually refer to these families because of their importance to the village through their trades. They tended to be the most prosperous of the families and could afford the gravestones. One such family were the Hobbs, who were the village carpenters and weavers until under ten years ago. The documentary record is often the only one for many of them. Although there were more than sixty members of the family buried in the churchyard, according to the registers we only have surviving gravestones for sixteen, and without the documentary record there would actually be very little detail of many of them.'

Tombstones of
Hobbs family

RON HOBBS

'I remember grandfather very well, he was very good to me as a schoolboy. I remember he bought me my first bicycle, yes.

' "In remembrance of Isaac Hobbs", that was my grandfather. He started the first business at Breamore. There was a lot of work done there, before harvest time there were as many as perhaps twenty wheels to be repaired. The farmers used to bring them in before the harvest you see so that they be ready in time to carry in the food produce and so on. He was the wheelwright, but of course after the last war tractors came in and then a lot of the farmers they had their wagons converted to rubber wheels to go behind the tractor, you see, and therefore in my time there wasn't so much wheelwrighting done.'

TONY LIGHT

'Another craft family within the village were the Edsalls, who were to become the village blacksmiths in the eighteenth century. About 1753 one of the Edsall family moved to a forge near the Marsh and this was the start of the blacksmith business. The

*forge today is still actually being run by a direct descendant of
the family, although the one at the Marsh closed some years ago
and now operates as a motor-mower repair shop.'*

TREVOR
KIMBER
(blacksmith)

*'There were four uncles, and I can remember all them working at
the different shops, the one at Downton and the one here and the
one at Alderholt, the other uncle he most of the time worked
with uncle Les in this shop, he didn't have a blacksmith's shop
on his own, he worked for this one.'*

*'I'm probably the last one of the family still doing this type of
work. What happens after that, well . . . I wouldn't be sure.'*

NORMAN
DYMOTT
Plaque on
ground: 'Lesley
Edsall'

*'This is a cremation we had here of two brothers which were
blacksmiths, one in our village and one at Downton. Lesley, the
one here, I know very very well, was a great character in the
village and always a great friend of the publican because he was
a frequent visitor there and his favourite saying was always when
you went in, "Well, are you going to buy one?" But he was a
wonderful character and many a tale he's told in the pub used to
keep the whole place in roars of laughter.'*

Leslie Edsall drank with Stanley Hall
though those who drank with Les bought all the beers.
Blacksmith and miller at the Bat and Ball
drinking to precarious careers.

Houses, one
with 'for sale'
sign

Wheelwright's and blacksmith's workshops both are sold,
each a des. res. and the sequestered vale
as each craftsman's like the miller's curfew's tolled
is less and less sequestered and for sale.

For Stanley Hall they're knotting their black ties,
they're buffing their black shoes to mirror shine.
With him some more of Breamore village dies,
he was the Breamore miller last in line.

Bearers load
coffin on to
hearse

For Stanley Hall they've brought the big black hearse,
buffed like their black shoes to high-gloss shine
to be taken to a grave without a verse.
If the job of miller's dated, so is mine.

NORMAN
DYMOTT

*'The majority of the people that's buried here are parishioners
and you've lived with them and been brought up with them and
therefore you know there's a personal touch in them, and it's a*

TONY HARRISON

lovely feeling that you can still walk back into your old village church and churchyard and find that your old relatives and workmates are still there with you.'

JOHN SHERING   *'I don't know what would happen now if someone was seen carrying a coffin through the town at dusk, but everything seemed normal then.'*

[Funeral procession]

VICAR   *'I am the Resurrection and the life, saith the Lord: he that believeth in me, though he were dead, yet shall he live: and whosoever liveth and believeth in me shall never die.'*

'I know that my Redeemer liveth, and that he shall stand at the latter day upon the earth: And though after my skin worms destroy this body, yet in my flesh shall I see God: whom I shall see for myself, and mine eyes shall behold, and not another.'

'O remember not the sins and offences of my youth but according to thy mercy think thou upon me O Lord for thy goodness' sake.'

Stanley Hall on photo

This was the Stanley Hall who made girls cry,
this is Stanley Hall in choirboy's gear
escorting a coffin from the days gone by
of solid elm, not mass-made and veneer.

Mourners and Vicar round grave, coffin lowered

Mr Trim's at his friend Stanley's head.
He'll be back home in time to feed his geese.
The man he drank his bitter with is dead,
the Breamore miller's gone to rest in peace.

A country churchyard burial in times
when most end up as ashes in cheap urns.
Pity the miller's headstone won't have rhymes,
quatrains as antiquated as his querns.

VICAR   *'We commend unto thy hands of mercy most merciful Father the soul of this our brother Charles Stanley Hall departed and we commit his body to the ground; earth to earth, ashes to ashes dust to dust . . .'*

78

And white dust gathers on the mill's grindstones.
Next year the miller Stanley will be mute
with forebears layered below already bones
when Breamore blesses Harvest flowers and fruit.

VICAR   *'. . . ever and ever, AMEN.'*

The village's last miller's in his hole
that the village's last sexton's got to fill,
The thudding sods begin their grim drum roll
and new commuters eye the empty mill.

One dying trade inters a now dead trade
and one by one the craftsmen pass away.
Soon the miller's grindstone and the sexton's spade
will be in John's museum for display.

NORMAN   *'He's just part of the village and that's it. The village . . . cricket*
DYMOTT   *. . . shooting – he was a very keen shot and a good shot too, old*
         Stan's one of the real old timers and very very sadly missed. Very
         sorry to think we're here today to do it.'

Some other local sits in Stanley's pew.
Someone else does his churchwarden's chores
and men from outside Breamore come to 'view'
will find Stan's footprints on the floury floors.

Congregation   *'. . . raise the song of harvest-home*
               All is safely gathered in,
               Ere the winter . . .'

There'll be one rusty voice, one Amen less
when all is safely gathered in again
and the folk of Breamore hear their rector bless
grapes freighted in from Italy or Spain.

'. . . come to God's own temple, come;
Raise the song of harvest-home.'

TONY HARRISON

'Oft did the harvest to their sickle yield,
Their furrow oft the stubborn glebe has broke;
How jocund did they drive their team afield!
How bow'd the woods beneath their sturdy stroke!

Let not Ambition mock their useful toil,
their homely joys, and destiny obscure;
Nor Grandeur hear with a disdainful smile,
The short and simple annals of the poor.

The boast of heraldry, the pomp of pow'r,
And all that beauty, all that wealth e'er gave,
Awaits alike th' inevitable hour.
The paths of glory lead but to the grave.'

Children singing   'It's the hard knock life for us
It's the hard knock life for us
Steada treated
We get tricked
Steada kisses
We get kicked
It's the hard-knock life.'

'Got no folks to speak of so
It's the hard-knock row we hoe
Cotton blankets
Steada wool
Empty bellies
Steada full
It's the hard-knock life.'

'Don't it feel like the wind is always howlin,
Don't it seem like there's never any light?
Once a day don't you wanna throw the towel in?
It's easier than putting up a fight.'

'No one's there when your dreams at night get creepy
No one cares if you grow or if you shrink
No one dries when your eyes get wet an weepy . . .

. . . it's a hard knock life.'

Mimmo Perrella non è Piu

Bay of Naples

Vesuvius and Naples, and the shore,
and a sky that, unpolluted, would be blue.

Death-bed scene

Mimmo Perrella non è piu.
Mimmo Perrella is no more.

Cemetery gates:
Tony Harrison
reads from
Death notice

Mimmo Perrella non è piu.
Mimmo Perrella is no more.
This gate his body will be carried through
he walked past into work not days before.

Mimmo Perrella non è piu.
Let's follow Mimmo Perrella's fate,
or, rather, not one single fate but two,
that of the body brought in through this gate

and put under marble in a dark, dry hole
where Vesuvius's soil makes it like leather,
and that other fate, meanwhile, of Mimmo's soul
exposed to an uncertain, otherworldly weather.

White marble
tombs

Mimmo's corpse stays here; his soul's set free
from the confines of its clay-stained cage
to struggle upwards, first to Purgatory
and after, Paradise, the final stage.

Stage one is when a man like Mimmo's died
and gets buried. Elsewhere that would be it.
But here in Naples when the body's dried
it gets dug up again out of its pit.

Poggioreale
Cemetery

Death, burial, exhumation, and then wound
in a winding sheet and put away
into a marble locker till the sound
of trumpets calling all to Judgement Day.

'Street' in
cemetery

It's only here in Naples that they do
the sorts of things at death that we'll see done.

Mimmo Perrella non è piu.

81

TONY HARRISON

Black horses and
carriage

It's starting now, his funeral. Stage One.

Baroque black coach, six horses from the stable
of Gaetano Bellomunno, undertaker.
In Naples only Bellomunno's able
to send you in such style to meet your Maker.

How many million *lire*? The 1.5
the family spent on such panache and state
they'd think a waste on Mimmo when alive
but once he's dead they never hesitate.

Coffin loaded on
to coach

A coach with gold rosettes and fleur-de-lys,
black and baroque, not British and discreet.
A funeral here's for everyone to see.
A Naples funeral brings out all the street.

Some get close, but others aren't so brave.
Some cope by unconcern. That man in grey,
while others maybe touch the box or wave,
can't face up to death, and turns away.

Coffin taken into
church

The censer swinging on the creaking chain,
the sobbing of a loved one half-suppressed,
commend the corpse of Mimmo freed from pain
to the care of God, and everlasting rest.

Coffin arrives at
Poggioreale
cemetery

Vesuvius, now calm since it erupted
in '44, when Mimmo was a boy.
Sirens, war, volcanoes never interrupted
the sort of sleep these 'dear deceased' enjoy.

And only one sound penetrates that sleep
though families come here frequently to pray
for their repose, have conversations, weep,
and that's the trumpet call to Judgement Day.

The Naples traffic scarcely ever stops.
They speed through green lights and ignore the red.
An ambulance with siren whining, cops,
might bring it to a halt. So will the dead.

82

Confraternity
Chapel: burial

Interred in *terra santa* for a span
of twenty or so months until it's dried
and what goes under marble as a man
comes out as Mimmo still, but mummified.

Then the desiccating soil is shovelled in,
when the marble slab's slid back in place,
that's the moment Mimmo's spirit must begin
its lengthy journey to the Lord's embrace.

And the family have to help to get him there.
Their love and care must will him on his way.
Spirit and corpse need suffrage and need prayer
and though he's more than missed he mustn't stay.

Though there's no sham about it when they grieve
and Mimmo's death broke everybody's heart,

Slab slid back
into place

the prayers they make encourage him to leave.
They need their 'dear departed' to depart.

Flower sellers

Souls make demands in dreams, but don't ask much,
a *rifresco*, a refreshment, some small treat,
flowers, a few words, to keep in touch
until that day when all of them will meet.

Basement of
S. Francesco
Bonifaco
Risorgeremo

RISORGEREMO carved above the door
by which the dead announce: *We shall arise.*
Though those the living visit are 'no more',
neither wants to break their family ties.

The conversations look a bit one-sided
but they seem to think their words get understood,
the phrase of love, the secret wish confided.
The dialogue's one way but does them good.

People tending
graves and
sitting quietly

'You've left our world and go towards another.
Though we're sorry that you've left us we're afraid
that what we loved as father, or grandmother,
might still turn back and haunt us as a shade.'

TONY HARRISON

Lockers where corpses crumble, skulls go hollow,
while the spirit labours slowly to its goal.
'Blaze a trail': she prays 'for me to follow':
'Show me the way when Death unlocks my soul.'

S. Giovanni a
Carbanara,
Confraternity
Chapel of Santa
Monica

The confraternity, the family and friends
and Monsignor Petrone, the same priest
who commended Mimmo's body, now commends
the *soul* of one less recently deceased.

Giuseppe Venturelli non è piu.
He's between his burial and exhumation.
His journey's almost two thirds through
and the mass will help him to his destination.

The confraternity is gathered for a mass
to help Giuseppe's spirit, and unite
their prayers and will to urge his soul to pass
from fire and darkness to the final light.

[Italian, with subtitles:]
*'We offer to God our supplications and the sacrifice of his own Son
so that, if there remains in Giuseppe any debt of sin, Divine mercy
will absolve it to let him reach the holy presence of God.'*

Priest, maestro, cello, keyboard, violin
urge Giuseppe's soul to new endeavour.
Once the hovering spirit's purged of sin
it won't be long before it's safe forever . . .

Cemetery Office:
Giovanni Errico
picks up tools

Giovanni takes the irons he needs to prise
the marble slab back open, dig, and bring
the body back before its loved ones' eyes,
not what went under but some other thing,

still with a person's features here and there,
a wizened replica of what they knew
with clothes that have rotted and with ragged hair,
the marks of one now many months *non piu.*

84

MIMMO PERRELLA NON È PIU

If when it's exhumed the body's wet
Giovanni's going to put the corpse back in.
It means the soul's not made it up there yet:
moistness, as of blood and sex, means sin.

Exhumation

Vincenzo Cicatiello non è piu.
He's been underground about two years.
When Mimmo Perrella's exhumation's due
his wife will greet him from the earth with tears.

He always took such trouble with his hair,
Even towards the end he kept it trim.
He was a natty dresser, took great care
over his appearance. Now, look at him!

First alcohol's sloshed on to wash him clean
then disconnected bones are put to rights,
then liberal sprinklings of naphthalene,
then DDT to keep off flies and mites.

Was this the Vincenzo who I slept beside?
Vincenzo Cicatiello non è piu.
Now, now I know you've really died.
Till now I only half-believed it true.

Being seen in such revolting tatters
wouldn't suit him. He was much too proud!
Although he's dead, she still believes it matters
that they make him feel he looks right in his shroud.

It took Vincenzo sixty years of life
and twenty months of death to look like this.
When they exhume her husband Mimmo's wife
will gaze on a flaking skull she used to kiss.

Giovanni carries
body covered
with black cloth

Under a blanket with a yellow cross
he clutches a crucifix in leather claw
and leaves a wife and sister with the wounds of loss
that won't heal till they too are 'no more'.

Puts body into
locker

Family mourning now's allowed to cease.
The 'dear departed' 's really left the scene.
The soul's in Purgatory, the corpse at peace
in his locker, talced with naphthalene.

Giovanni
stacking coffins
into incinerator

Though his father dug up bodies in the past
and generation hands it down to generation,
Giovanni hopes that he's the last
and Neapolitans accept cremation.

Though cremation has no popular approval
and might take years of work to win their hearts
when even after surgical removal
they won't incinerate the cankered parts;

a hysterectomy, an amputation,
a liver or a kidney cut away,
even these aren't given a cremation
but get put into the soil till Judgement Day,

when everything that's rotten is restored,
soul, head, body, arms, legs, feet.
No one expects to limp up to the Lord
or be resurrected only half-complete.

Coffins burning

In Naples only coffins get cremated.
As the corpse's empty box goes in the flame,
to reach that Paradise so long awaited
the soul in Purgatory goes through the same.

Skulls and bones
in the Fontanelle

With family help Vincenzo's made it there
and in Purgatory his soul will get its purging.
But what of those who get no family care,
who got no mass, no prayers, no loved ones' urging?

Mimmo, Giuseppe, Vincenzo, all those three
have wives and families who'll do their best
to ensure that they'll get through to Purgatory,
and after a brief purging, join the blessed.

Perhaps the Plague or epidemic dropped
so many bony orphans in one place
for Neapolitans to pity and adopt
and for refreshment given get back grace.

These are souls who don't have Mimmo's luck
and are abandoned and so can't aspire
to Blessedness above, and they stay stuck
in transit in the Purgatorial fire.

If prayer can ease the purifying blaze,
give balm to the abandoned where they burn,
their gratitude to someone when he prays
comes back as graces granted in return.

And those who grant such grace might get a niche.
to keep the favours flowing, for repose,
though which old rib bone once belonged to which,
which skull to which stray hip, nobody knows.

Pray for the dead, the Catholic priests exhort,
but these popular beliefs are thought to border
on black magic, not what the Church has taught.
So the ossuary got closed by priestly order.

Rafaelle's tomb,
Enzo praying

Those abandoned souls in Fontanelle
are unreachable with bonehouse entrance bricked,
but there's the famous tomb of Rafaelle
that Enzo Borelli discovered derelict.

To show what abandoned souls can do
when given favours let's look at the story
of one over a century *non piu* –
Rafaelle Liberatore . . .

Enzo Borelli restored his tomb and gates
and heaps the once neglected spot with flowers
and Rafaelle, pleased, recriprocates
by transmitting through Borelli healing powers.

TONY HARRISON

	[Italian with subtitles:]
Blond woman	*'I've come here for fifteen years and had many requests granted. A few days ago, my husband couldn't piss – The doctor wanted to do tests – but that night I put a photo of Rafaele on his stomach and next morning, he did 800 grams of urine . . . without doing the tests, or taking pills.'*
Grey-haired woman	*'I wanted a job for my son: within a year he found one.'*
Blond woman	*'Enzo is very important, he makes requests for us and recieves signs. He explains them and everything he says is true. That's why Enzo is so important.'*

Enzo praying,
women praying
and watching

All these flowers, this *rifresco* giving
earned for Enzo Rafaelle's first known grace –
Enzo's sick mama continued living
when doctors had pronounced a hopeless case.

Enzo the rubber prays to Rafaelle
who's been 'no more' since 1853.
His photo on an ailing hubby's belly
guarantees 800 grams of pee;

Women rubbing
marble face

work for a son, fiancé for a daughter,
a once abandoned soul grants all this grace –
making money, making progress, making water
come from rubbing Rafaelle's marble face.

He wrote verses too. I wouldn't mind
being like Rafaelle when I die,
a woman stroking me then her behind,
first fingering my face, and then her thigh –

Enzo kisses
marble face of
Rafaelle

but I wouldn't fancy smackers from this guy!

Mimmo Perrella non è piu,
the years will pass, his soul get nearer heaven.
His corpse put in its locker after two
will still get visits after six or seven.

Giovanni Errico
takes bodies of
Vincenzo and
Titina Genovese
out of marble
'locker',
unwraps
winding sheet,
cleans and dusts
bones

My father died some seven years ago
and once he'd gone my Mamma couldn't wait
for the marble slab that Babba lay below
to be slid back for her to share his fate.

Souls make demands in dreams but don't ask much,
a *rifresco*, a 'refreshment', some small treat,
the locker opened for a loved one's touch,
a dusting down, a change of winding sheet.

It's not the Church but love says that I must.
And it's something that I'll always come to do,
till either they've both crumbled into dust
or I'm in the locker with them and *non piu*.

Portions of a person gnawed by mites,
this carcase crumbling limb by leather limb,
the leather liver, leather lungs and lights . . .
I still find my father in what's left of him.

Picks up hand

This hand that patted me, or, once or twice,
gave me an angry clout across the head.
My parents' spirits, safe in Paradise,
still like to see their bits in the same bed.

Wraps bodies in
clean sheets,
replaces in
locker

I've had, you'd think, quite long enough to grieve.
They've both been dead for almost seven years.
I find it hard to take a final leave
or notice that they're missing without tears.

Two medallions in marble, some loose bones,
where parents whose embrace made me had been.
But a son can't show his love if he disowns
these fragments bundled up in naphthalene.

To know we'll meet in Heaven makes me glad.
Babba, Mama, are both now *non piu*
but we'll be back together when they add
non è piu to their son Enzo too.

And when Enzo Genovese *non è piu*
this is the locker he will go inside
and his spirit will be smelling the *ragu*
his mother made each Sunday till she died.

All Souls' Day The afterlife means family, hugging, kissing,
the table set for everlasting dinner
with all their loved ones round it, no one missing
and no one diseased or sick, or still a sinner.

And All Souls' Day's a carnival of caring
for all those who've gone before and for their tombs.
Remembering bereavements they come bearing
bunches of gladioli and bright blooms

for all their loved ones, and a few
for graves no one's brought flowers for.
Three million in this place are *non piu*
and before the day is over there'll be more.

Procession and But though people die today, because of crowds
crowds there'll be no funeral coaches at the gate,
there'll be no burials, no change of shrouds
and souls bound for beyond will have to wait.

And the Cardinal will come arrayed in red
to walk past in procession and to pray
and give his blessing to three million dead
who wait as bones and dust for Judgement Day.

The All Souls' Day traffic's far too thick,
the ambulance we hear just can't get through.
Before it manages to reach whoever's sick
another Neapolitan *non è piu*.

Relax in your marble lockers you who wait
the call to Judgement Day, this isn't it.
Another man, like Mimmo, 's met his fate
and soon he'll start to dry out in his pit,

while his soul has other voyages to start
towards a place you can't get to alive,
and though most souls seem reluctant to depart
they're happier than here once they arrive.

So Neapolitans believe with few exceptions.
I'm the odd one out in disbelief.
But if they fool themselves, then the deception's
at least a healing way to handle grief.

And all these visitors this All Souls' Day
bringing their flowers to honour those who've gone
will come to the cemetery one day to stay
and start the journey Mimmo's started on.

And if you were a believer, unlike me,
and you looked towards Vesuvius, Capri,
the curving bay, the ocean, would you see
the souls of the departed passing through
the pall of pollution over Napoli,
through chemicals and clouds into the blue . . .

And beyond maybe? All I know is true:

Espedito Saggiomo non è piu

Vincenzo Genovese non è piu

Titina Genovese non è piu

Rafaelle Liberatore non è piu

Vincenzo Cicatiello non è piu

Giuseppe Ventorelli non è piu

Mimmo Perrella non è piu

Cheating the Void

Oblivion is darkness, Memory light.
They're locked in eternal struggle. Which
of these two forces really shows its might
when death's doors are thrown open by a switch?

Archive film:
workers coming
out of factory,
1895

These people are all dead, and yet they walk.
The first in fact to move on celluloid.
Though they are silent and won't ever talk
their very movements seemed to cheat the void.

Death's no longer absolute, wrote the reviewer
having seen this film in 1895.
Do our TVs and videos make that truer
and help to make the dead seem more alive?

[PARIS: PERE LACHAISE]

Out of the Metro to the upper air
the dead brought back from underneath the ground,
and a century since the film of Lumière
out of the Metro, coloured, and with sound.

Napoleonic Paris cleared its plague-filled tombs
and first showed Europe more hygienic ways.
They stacked the dug-up bones in catacombs
and opened a green place called Père Lachaise.

Paris pushed, promoted and PRed
to induce the city's dead to settle there
and re-buried Héloise with Abelard
and brought in La Fontaine and Molière,

and by process of promotional exhumation
of endorsing heroes long ago decayed
lured both great and small to emulation –
and now draws TV crews and tourist trade.

TONY HARRISON

Tour starts
The tour starts here with voices in your head.
Hear one corpse sing what another corpse composes.
Follow their music, let yourself be led
to where the shell of genius reposes.

Composers rot but their recorded notes
are all we need to make them seem alive.
The singers buried here have crumbled throats
but the voices they vibrated with survive.

And that, what's that? . . . A bird?
Follow the leafy paths to track the sound
and maybe find it's not a thrush you heard
but Mez Mezzrow's clarinet from underground.

Chopin's tomb,
with tourists
The Muse, one of Memory's nine daughters
looks and doesn't like what she beholds,
the lyre finally unstrung when Lethe's waters
took Chopin underneath her chilly folds.

Drawn down into Oblivion and drowned
in Eternity's white noise and endless hiss
from where the waves wash up the surfaced sound
of divas from the same dark depths, like this.

Bellini's tomb
Adelina Patti, Callas and the former
from scratchy wax before the First World War
sings 'Casta Diva' from Bellini's *Norma*
then Callas, on hissless tracks, gives an encore.

Offspring of Edison's first phonograph,
intended by him only for dictation,
enables us to listen to Piaf
and engineer her vocal exhumation.

Oblivion that all our art defies.
Oblivion where all of us must go.
Oblivion that's gazed on by the eyes
Géricault's tomb of this graveyard's greatest painter, Géricault

who went on painting till the very last
defying the dark void through his last days
till he changed his pain-racked body for one cast
in bronze still painting here in Père Lachaise.

Bronze relief of
*The Raft of the
Medusa*

His masterwork *The Raft of the Medusa*,
blown by the wind and battered by the waves,
reproduced in metal but its sculptor/reproducer
believing no male organ much suits graves

Jim Morrison's
tomb

made the dying man more modest for the frieze
and gave the death-offending member a bronze veil.
But *Jim* who doesn't, *didn't*, care who sees,
for unveiling his on stage, got thrown in gaol.

'Death and my cock are the world,' said Jim.
That may have been but now I rather doubt
there's much left of that vaunted part of him
or nothing that he'd feel like pulling out.

[LONDON: KENSAL GREEN, NUNHEAD]

The void may well be cheated by a voice,
composer's quill, the artist's brush or pen,
but memory might only have one choice:
a stone in Kensal Green – £11.10.

Mr Kemp, the mason, Kensal Green,
professional friend to loving memory,
of the firm of J. S. Farley who have been
naming the void since 1833:

MR KEMP

*'Here are some of the books which were used in those days as
catalogues with hand-painted drawings of the various memorials.
These are round about the 1850s. There is a tomb there, £55,
inscription extra. There's one here in Portland stone, a solid tomb,
£11 10s, inscription extra. There's a six-foot headstone there
curbing and foot stone, £11 11s. Another one for £11 10s, £6 15s
6d.*

Memory puts up names in chiselled letters
meant to last beyond the mourners' day;
Oblivion makes descendants soon forget us
and lets the weather wear the names away.

The spider spinning on the holly bough,
the moths that spiral in the shafts of sun
are all the visitors the dead get now
where Memory's strangled by Oblivion.

The stone that still reads WATSON's going green.
Lichen furs the letters of each word.
Crevasses to be crossed are all they mean
to millipede and ant and ladybird.

The first Oblivion is death, the next
neglect, and finally the third
where moss and ivy blank out mason's text
and no one cares whose body is interred.

Vandals might strip tombstones of their lead,
jerk ring or jewelled bangle off a bone,
of value to the living not the dead,
but Oblivion can do such work alone.

MR KEMP
(echoed)

'£11 11s . . . £6 15s 6d . . . £55 . . . £11 10s . . . Inscription extra.'

Bodies with breeding, a better class of bone
first drew dead clientele to Kensal Green
which claimed a royal corpse to set the tone.
A princess made it *the* place to be seen.

This, as Mr Kemp would say, 's a 'solid tomb',
one of the first and solidest erected here
and the deferential swish of worker's broom
keeps common dust from settling on Sophia.

Sophia, daughter of King George III
(though 'precedence beneath the earth's a jest!'),
by choosing Kensal Green to be interred
gave it the cachet to attract the best.

Lords and Ladies, late and early nipped
beneath heartsease, forget-me-not and yew.
What are they now, a stone with chiselled script
saying SIR WILLIAM CASEMENT – who?

Late of Bengal but now of Kensal Green,
Sir William Casement oversees these kids,
jobless for a year, employed to clean
his lichen-encrusted caryatids.

Chuprassie, sepoy, subahdar,
used to serve Sir William's slightest whim.
Now, things being in Britain what they are,
these have no choice but bow and scrape to him.

The circus owner joins the social set.
Though the nobs are no doubt snubbing him in
    Heaven
Ducrow's bones are rubbing shoulders with Debrett
for 300 times '£11. 11.' –

('*Inscription extra*'.)

Pegasus the winged horse helps him fly,
this 'Colossus of Equestrians' Ducrow
without his hat and gloves into the sky,
and angels from the next tomb watch his show.

Before the Blesseds' astonished saintly faces
Ducrow still cracks his circus master's whips,
putting God's chariot horses through their paces
and the spangled Horsemen of the Apocalypse.

[GENOA: STAGLIENO]

Ducrow dismounts where bourgeois Genoese
made monuments more lavish than his own,
the chiselling bankers' chiselled effigies,
the solid burghers even solider in stone.

TONY HARRISON

Mazzini buried here serenely stated
(before he died) that Death did not exist.
Others hedge their bets and get translated
from flesh into marble by a realist.

Flesh perishes but marble's meant to last.
They squandered money they'd amassed by trade
to cut a dash in death, not be outclassed
by competition in the colonnade.

Not just a hat and gloves as with Ducrow
but *them*, their face, their limbs, and what they wore,
not just on top but all the frills below
and every detail etched cried out for more –

the delicate brocade, the flimsy lace,
the widow's teardrop falling from a lash,
every feature Memory could trace
provided the remembered had the cash.

Tomb of
nutseller

I didn't have it, but I swore I would.
I'd save my *lire* so that when I died
I'd stand among the nobs. I'm just as good
though they sniff a bit to see me at their side.

They don't like hawkers in the colonnade
and I sold necklaces of nuts and rings of bread.
Though alive they might despise my lowly trade
they can't feel quite so snooty when they're dead.

Coin by coin commissioned, head to toe,
the nutseller enshrined among the rich,
not sorry to take my rest from life below,
glad that my marble twin still works my pitch.

I worked too hard to have kids of my own
and having kids is all I'd say I miss.
I feel a wee bit jealous when that child of stone
gives her mamma a long, lingering kiss.

CHEATING THE VOID

[SOUTH OF FRANCE: MARSEILLE, NICE]

Sunshine is life and here the Sunny Med
with honeymooners, beachballs and blue sky
seems an unlikely landscape for the dead,
but even the idle rich have got to die.

The best of life so close, so out of reach.
How tantalizing to be good and dead
with all those sunburnt bodies on the beach
when you're mere marble, and no eyes in your head.

The sun, the sea, the half-clad shapes,
topless torsos, thighs lapped by the waves,
all have a date with death no one escapes,
stretched out, as if to sunbathe, in their graves.

They see them sunbathe, and they see them swim
if a dead man's eyesight can survive.
So much *joie de vivre*, and yet, says Jim,
NO ONE HERE GETS OUT ALIVE!

Jim Morrison synch.

OK Jim, but there's no need to shout.
Go back and rest your bones in Père Lachaise.
Everybody knows they won't get out
of here alive, but like their holidays.

These waters, so inviting in the sun,
that people dip their toes in, swim in, float,
can darken any day into Oblivion
and a farewell sail in Charon's ferry boat.

[VENICE: SAN MICHELE]

This island of the dead's so short of space,
most graves in Venice have a ten-year lease
then each cross with the dead's ceramic face
gets moved, and those who want to rest in peace

get their bones collected for the common pile
to make room for another boat-borne box.
The dead spared exhumation on this isle
are the famous and the Russian Orthodox

which include Stravinsky and Diaghilev.
Our sound machine exhumes their *Rite of Spring*
to summon flowers up. The dead are deaf
to music, birdsong, boats, to everything;

to these drums that shake the earth down to its core,
invoking spring to turn the dug soil green,
to the furiously following First World War
shaking all the cemeteries we've seen.

[MILAN: CIMITERO MONUMENTALE]

Time running out for Europe and for man,
Oblivion in our century overtaking
Memory, pursued here to Milan
where men of stone bring God's heart close to
                                    breaking.

What does Christ gaze down on from his cross?
A century where innocence has died
and mankind finds no meaning in the loss
of millions almost worse than crucified.

Child (Mia)
alongside tomb
sculpture of
child

Film machines exhume the ones who've died
and bring this baby Mia back to view
but Oblivion with his bombs and genocide
is almost neck and neck since World War II.

Innocence all unaware how time
can make her smiling playmates petrified.
Graves are fun to play on and to climb,
she doesn't know the meaning of 'they died'.

Locked in eternal struggle which one wins,
Oblivion or Memory, Darkness, Light?
Maybe Oblivion and Memory are twins

Photos of twins

like here on this gravestone, left and right.

Machines have maximized Oblivion's slaughter
that Memory films on Lumière's machine
and this Muse in Milan here, Memory's daughter
doesn't seem to care for what she's seen.

That emotion in the Muse's face is fear
that shows itself through her half-covered eyes
as the century darkens over baby Mia
and Oblivion's smoke stacks blacken Europe's skies.

[HAMBURG: OHLSDORF]

Herr Blümke
walking in
cemetery,
shooting rabbits

This bloke in case you think so's not recruiting.
Graveyards don't have problems keeping full.
It's not a human enemy he's shooting,
it's Herr Blümke's early-morning rabbit cull.

The dead don't register the rifle's sound,
though once for days on end that's all they heard,
burrowing for their lives into the ground.
Now rabbits burrow down where they're interred.

Herr Blümke, rabbit culler, takes the prize –
2,000 killed a year here, but the War
when it came rabbiting to Hamburg from the skies
in just one day bagged 50,000 more!

Archive film of
charred bodies
lying in street

We'd sooner that Oblivion destroyed
some memories like these Hamburg streets.
Some film we'd sooner pitch into that void
that Lumière's invention sometimes cheats.

In 1943 the Allied raid
intended to subdue the German nation
caused fires that reached 800 centigrade,
200 more than needed for cremation.

The lawns of Ohlsdorf, where still mourning mothers
search level grass, where every loved one shares
a common grave with 50,000 others
but want to claim one blade of it as theirs.

'Remember me, but, ah, forget my fate!'
Impossible in Hamburg. History refuses
to have that motto carved above her gate
as she's the least forgiving of the Muses.

TONY HARRISON

Gates of
Bombenopfer
monument open
to reveal
Charon's ferry

The gates of death are opening once more
not to let souls out, as in the Lumière,
but into Charon's ferry for the farther shore.
He starts the outboard with a stony stare.

Why do the ferried close their chiselled eyes?
What do you passengers not want to see?
Their destination where dark Oblivion lies
or what they leave behind in Germany?

Charon's ferry's chugging at the wharf
for those who do not care for what they've seen
from this landing stage of stone here at Ohlsdorf,
from Venice, Genoa, Milan, and Kensal Green,

from Nunhead, Menton and from Père Lachaise,
but Charon's eyes are never known to close.
He sees the sad processions and his gaze
pierces Oblivion's depths like Géricault's.

Tours go back to where they started,
always A to A not A to Z,
but in this ferry boat once you've departed
Charon chugs back empty for more dead.

Letters in the Rock

LADY ROSE
HARE

'*We don't really know what sort of person she was, what her interests were or anything like that.*'

VICKY NAISH

'*I mean he's, he's still my dad as far as I'm concerned, he'll never be any different.*'

MYRA DAVEY

'*They loved their garden, they really did, and after they died the natural thing to do was to scatter their ashes in their garden.*'

THE HON.
SIMON
HOWARD

'*They'd put a lot back into Castle Howard and so it was a logical conclusion to their lives to be buried here in the Mausoleum.*'

MAUREEN
STREET

'*I mean he was only ten months old, he was quite fond of soft toys.*'

[MASTER MASONS' CONFERENCE, BLACKPOOL]

In Blackpool August 1936
Dad planted me inside my Mother's womb.
The fact of my conception's hard to mix
with letters etched by chisels on a tomb.

My father's favourite place for holidays
isn't the first place I'd expect to see
such mournful graveyard furniture displays,
the mason's trappings of mortality.

This stone that's aptly carved with Blackpool Tower
isn't just display, it waits the name
of one who's reached the inevitable hour
and thinks that Heaven and Blackpool are the same.

'In Loving
Memory of
Thomas Gray'
on computer
screen

'In Loving Memory of Thomas Gray.'
Good job the letters in it are a few –
sandblasted and then squirted with gold spray
each letter costs you £1.32.

TONY
HARRISON

Now we've got Thomas Gray, could we have a verse from Gray's Elegy?

TONY MILLS

Yes, in that style?

TONY
HARRISON

In that style, fine, if I can remember it.

TONY HARRISON

TONY MILLS	*Yes, we clear that one, quite logically from line one we can select this style and the text and the size that we need and quite simply type it in, so if you tell me what to type in, away we go.*
TONY HARRISON	*Right, 'The Boast of Heraldry . . .'*
SALES PERSON	*You see if you've got a very windy cemetery then you're going to find that that will stay within the container, no problem. Something like that in a very windy area with tall flowers and it's just going to blow over and you're not going to keep them there at all. That's the whole idea of the weight.*
CUSTOMER	*I see that . . .*
TONY HARRISON	*'. . . the Pomp of Pow'r* *And all that Beauty, all that Wealth e'er gave,'* *. . . new line –* *'Awaits alike th'inevitable Hour.* *The Paths of Glory lead but to the Grave.'*

It's shock enough to know your loved one's gone
but the mason estimating that the rock
your dear departed's name gets lettered on
will cost eight hundred pounds compounds the shock.

If memorials are raised the words are terse.
In Memory's sometimes shortened to I.M.
and almost no tombs now get lines of verse.
The paths of glory lead but to the crem.

In fire and molten magmas mountains started
and turned into granites ebony, red, grey,
that bear the chiselled names of our departed
that several lifespans shouldn't wear away.

Rock factory	Sugar and syrup at 300 Fahrenheit – poured on to metal plates this boiling mix of Blackpool magma cools to brilliant white coloured and lettered, cut into sweet licks.

The fates, those three that measure, spin and sever
on ancient looms or something up to date,
allot us all a span that's not for ever –
from the start life's lettered with our final fate.

VICAR in
crematorium

*Jesus said, I am the resurrection and the life, whoever believes in me
will live, even though he dies, and whoever lives and believes in me
will never die. Do not be worried and upset, he said. Believe in God
and believe in me. There are many mansions in my Father's house
and I am going to prepare a place for you.*

'Burning Burials', said Sir Thomas Browne,
stop 'our skulls being used as drinking bowls',
the puny and the portly rendered down
to about five pounds of powder, and their souls.

But there's the rub, for many are afraid
that souls don't stand much chance of coming
                                        through
a chamber where 600 centigrade
makes windblown ash of all the rest of you.

What Americans have christened 'the cremains'
poured through a plastic funnel to return
to nature, and tomorrow's autumn rains
wash away what's shaken from the urn.

'Slow thro' the Church-way Path we saw him borne'.
Gray's *Elegy*'s a mine of apt quotation
but an Elegy on a Crematorium Lawn
wasn't what fired Gray's imagination.

This is where they lead, the paths of glory,
and the British, on the whole, don't seem to care,
but let's let some who do tell us their story
of who they want remembered, how, and where:

MYRA DAVEY
(Myra's house,
Taunton)

*'When my father's parents both died they both wished that they
should be cremated so we did this. The service I thought was much
nicer and afterwards the question of the ashes. I said to father, well,
what shall we do with the ashes and you really didn't want anything
to remind you, did you?'*

ERNIE
HILLBURN

*'No, and my mother and father used to spend a lot of time in the
garden and Myra suggested scattering them in the garden which I
thought was a good idea.'*

MYRA DAVEY

*'They loved their garden, they really did, because Grandma always
used to refer to the bottom part of her garden as a 'little bit of
Heaven', and she always said that she felt nearer to God*

there than anywhere else, so when Grandpa died to me the natural thing was to put them together. I did it totally by myself. I did it late afternoon. It was an emotional thing for me because I felt I'd brought them home again and there, that is where they were going to stay.'

ERNIE
HILLBURN

'You see, the cemeteries in the course of time they get very neglected and there comes a time when I'm gone and probably my daughter's gone, and nobody else will ever go to the grave or to care for it and then it just goes derelict.'

MYRA DAVEY

'Of course at Taunton Deane they've got the facility of the Book of Remembrance and both my grandparents' names are there and my Mother's name will be put there.'

ERNIE
HILLBURN

'We go out every anniversary to read – to look at the book – to read their names.'

MYRA DAVEY

'To read their names, yes. We found that most, well everyone wishes cremation more than anything else. I myself, I would want it and I know that Dad certainly wants it.'

ERNIE
HILLBURN

'Oh yes . . . yes, I should definitely want to be cremated.'

MYRA DAVEY

'Yes.'

ERNIE
HILLBURN

'And I don't mind what they . . .'

MYRA DAVEY

'What's done with you. (Laughs.) You'll probably end up in the garden. Oh, you like your garden, Dad. (Laughs.)'

VICKY NAISH
(Nunhead
Cemetery)

'We much prefer burials, this is our way of thinking. My father's wish was always to be buried, always. He always said never burn me, Vicky, you know, because he was burned enough in the War, you know, and he never ever approved of cremations, always burials, much preferred burials. And he's got his wish. This is not a private grave, it's a public grave, which was my mother's wish, to have an ordinary common grave, for the simple reason before my father died at the beginning of 1982 Nunhead Cemetery was in the news quite a lot about vandalism, people coming into the cemetery and opening the old graves. Because many years ago, and it still sticks in my Mum's mind, if you had a big headstone and a private grave and so forth that meant you had plenty of money and you were actually buried with all your jewels etc. So we much prefer to have it this way and to have a wooden cross and not only that, there's not just my father buried here, there are five others, because

Vicky tidying
grave

normally a common grave has six coffins, you know, six people in it. I mean I don't know who the other five are. When I first used to visit the first Christmas there was somebody else attending to this* *grave as well, but unfortunately I haven't seen anybody now for at least two years that come up here to see to it, just my family, my Mum and myself and my husband. And that's all.'*

'You never forget someone who's so important to you, I mean every day there's something that goes on that clicks through your mind that, oh, you know, even if you're on a bus or something like that, you'll just look out of the bus window or even your home, you look out of the window, and you'll see sort of a thing, like a car or something like that – oh, my dad used to have one of those. Every day there's always something in life that reminds you of the dead.'

SIMON
HOWARD
(Castle Howard
Mausoleum)

'Well, here we are in the Chapel of the Mausoleum, which is in the main drum behind the columns and sits above the crypt. As you can see it's a very light and spacious and airy room. It was from here in front of the altar that the service was conducted for my father's funeral, with the clergy either side, whereas for my mother's funeral the service was conducted from inside this stall here. I think a rather more impressive position. And then the family would have sat in these pews either side – stalls. And they have a certain amount of depth to them and one really gets a feeling of space.'

Simon enters
crypt

'Well, this is the crypt which houses sixty-three niches and of these sixty-three, nineteen are permanently occupied by my forebears. It's down here in the crypt that the committal takes place and the body is in the coffin which is put into the niche, and once in the niche when everyone has gone the stone is put in place, and on that stone will be carved the name of the occupant, and the date of birth and death, and more often than not whose son or daughter they were.'

Simon and his
mother's and
father's niches

'Previous to this century the last person to be interred in the Mausoleum was the eighth Earl of Carlisle. He was interred in 1889 and it wasn't till my mother died in 1974 that the practice was started again. Both my mother and father felt very strongly that they had contributed a great deal to the resurrection of this estate and they both felt that they wanted to be buried together here in the Mausoleum. My father died in 1984 and was interred below my mother.'

'In the future it is hoped that all the family will continue to be buried here at the Mausoleum, certainly myself.'

MAUREEN
STREET
(Nunhead
cemetery, teddy-
bear grave)

'My dad did say to me, will you have him cremated, and I just said yes, yes, 'cause it was only sort of the day or the day after, and I'm really really pleased that Stephen, he just said no, no, and I didn't argue with him. I said, all right, if that's what you want. I just wanted it over and done with, but now I really am so glad that he's been buried rather than cremated. Can't imagine burning a baby's body, no matter if he's dead or what, you know.'

'We felt that a teddy bear would have been more appropriate for his age, because he was only a baby. An ordinary headstone, they cost so much money, and it wasn't what we wanted. I mean, they could have done us one on granite, as a headstone four or five inches thick with a teddy bear carved on it, which is not what we wanted. We wanted something that looked cuddly, that looked solid.'

STEPHEN
STREET

'Every time I look at it it breaks my heart, but if I went up there and looked at a lump of granite I don't suppose it would mean anything to me.'

MAUREEN
STREET

'I think it's made with love, where granite's made for profit. That teddy bear is made because I wanted to make it, I wanted to do something for him, and it's filled with love. I mean, to me that teddy bear is him really. He was cuddly and that's just how the teddy bear looks to me, you know. I mean sometimes I go up there and I expect it to be soft, but he's, I mean, it's hard as stone . . . (Laughs.)

I made it myself in an adult institute during the day, on a Monday afternoon, which took me quite some time, but I felt I was doing something for him and it kept me going. It really did keep me going. We thought the verse was very very appropriate, especially for a cot-death baby. It was,

"We were not there to see you die to hold your hand or say goodbye but we'll remember our whole lives through those ten short months we spent with you."

– and then I just put "God Bless'. He's my son, you know, and I feel very strongly about it, that I should give him some of my time, and an hour out of every two weeks doesn't hurt anybody. And I like him to have fresh flowers, it's the least I can do for him. The thought of him having dead flowers, you know, if they've been up there for a month or two, it really upsets me, so I like to go and replace them. Perhaps in years to come, when I'm over it a bit more, perhaps I'll plant flowers and then I'll know that he'll have fresh flowers, plants, and I won't need to go so much, but at the moment I still need to go that much. It's almost as if he's still with me, perhaps that's how I feel, you know, I won't let him go.'

SIR THOMAS HARE (Stow Bardolph Chapel, Norfolk) Children at Sunday School	'Well, the Chapel was built at the end of the sixteenth century and it's really the only thing that's left here which was contemporary with the first settlement of our family in the area. I often wonder what the people buried underneath would think about a lot of children running about over their corpses, but I like to think that they were all, nearly all of them were members of very big families, and I just hope that they would like the idea of the new life continuing.'
	'Quiet, quiet now, everybody, and let's all be quiet and remember where we are and we start as usual by saying the Lord's Prayer together: "Our Father which art in Heaven . . ." '
LADY ROSE HARE Monuments in Chapel	'We wanted to start a Sunday School and it was the only place that we could start it. We're very fond of the Chapel and especially since we've had the Sunday School, it's all come alive in a way.'
SIR THOMAS AND CHILDREN	' ". . . and deliver us from evil, for the Kingdom, the Power and the Glory are yours, now and for ever, Amen." '
SIR THOMAS	'Now, it's Catherine's turn this week to read a prayer, and when she's said it the response is, "Dear God, we believe in you." '
CATHERINE	'Dear God, thank you for all our friends and relations who have died, we are glad that you have made Heaven so that we don't have to be so sad. We know that you have room for every one who believes in you.'
SIR THOMAS AND CHILDREN	'Dear God, we believe in you.'
SIR THOMAS	'I should like the tradition of monuments to continue, in a simple form, but perhaps showing something about the person and their interests on them, as well as just the bare facts of when they were born and died. The only specific instruction I've left in my own will is that I should have a Christian burial because you never know, you might die in some part of the world where that wouldn't happen. I thought that was important.'
LADY ROSE	'Yes, I agree with Tom. I think I'd like some sort of memorial and I should like my interests shown on that memorial, maybe in some sort of decoration, just to show what sort of person one was a little bit. Not just one's name and age.'
Door opens to reveal wax effigy	'Now, we're going to open the cupboard and see who's come back. Shall we open it very slowly and see who's in there . . .'
CHILDREN	'Ooooooooo!'
LADY ROSE	'Now who can remember her here before?'

CHILDREN (arguing)	'No. yes.'
LADY ROSE	'What do you think's been happening to her while she's been away?'
SIR THOMAS	'Well this is the wax effigy of Sarah Hare, there are no other wax effigies as far as we know in parish churches in this country.'
LADY ROSE	'She does look a bit different, doesn't she?'
CHILD	'She looks much different, she had longer hair . . .'
LADY ROSE	'Do you think her hair looks different?'
CHILDREN	'Yes . . .
SIR THOMAS	'She left very specific instructions in her will. She says, "I desire to have my face and hands made in wax, with a piece of crimson satin thrown like a garment in a picture. Hair upon my head and put in a case of mahogany with a glass before and fixed up so near the place where my corpse lies as it can be, with my name and time of death put upon the case in any manner most desirable." '
LADY ROSE	'Do you think she's glad to be back? She died in 1744, so how old does that make her?'
CHILD	'About a thousand . . .'
LADY ROSE	'No, not quite as much as that.'

Clown laughing,
Blackpool

'The Boast of Heraldry, the Pomp of Pow'r
And all that Beauty, all that Wealth e're gave,
Awaits alike th' inevitable Hour.
The Paths of Glory lead but to the Grave.'

Blackpool for me's this clown convulsed with laughter
and how people on their holidays behave,
not the paraphernalia of the hereafter
and lettered rock that marks a person's grave,

The heraldry of Howard and of Hare,

Blackpool Tower
on gravestone of
Harold Marsden

the crem that burns up power, beauty, fame,
the baby's grave with home-made teddy bear,
and the tomb with Blackpool Tower that waits a name

Harold loved his Blackpool all year round
and what he loved in life he wanted after,
Blackpool Tower, the pier, the prom, the sound
of waves and gulls and fun and seaside laughter.

LADY   '*Give over, will you . . .*'

OTHER LADY   '*No, you've got to laugh . . .*'

Sings   '*. . . with my little stick
of Blackpool rock, along the
promenade I stroll . . .*'

Harold's gone to his Blackpool in the sky
and if, like him, my Blackpool-loving dad
had believed here's where we go to when we die
he wouldn't have thought that dying was too bad.

If when getting near the inevitable hour
my dad like Harold Marsden had have thought
that he'd need his pumps for foxtrots in the Tower,
he'd have packed less glumly for the last resort.

Life's stick of rock's still got a few sweet licks
and death lettered right through life can't make it sour,
so lick your skullicious lollies down to sticks
and scorn for now the inevitable hour.